HOW TO REST AUTO UPHOLSTERY

John Martin Lee

Motorbooks International
Publishers & Wholesalers ®

The hobby of restoring cars and trucks has spawned a great industry, supplying the material needs of those who engage in it. Many of those companies and clubs furnished information, samples, instructions and photographs which appear in this book. I am grateful to all of them.
I would especially like to thank Norm Kyhn of Kyhn's Kustom Krafts in Longmont, Colorado; Randy Vajgrt, Matt Swanson and Jack Compton at McVicker Auto Upholstery and Tops, and Ira Fazel, Moe Wilson and Kurt Riley of Ira's Upholstering Service, both of Lincoln, Nebraska. They allowed me to look over their shoulders, take pictures and ask questions as they went about their work of making old interiors new.
Thanks to Dave Brownell, editor of *Special Interest Autos*, who was kind enough to share the photos and information he had published on covering a padded dash.

First published in 1994 by Motorbooks International Publishers & Wholesalers, PO Box 2, 729 Prospect Avenue, Osceola, WI 54020 USA

Motorbooks International is a certified trademark, registered with the United States Patent Office

The information in this book is true and complete to the best of our knowledge. All recommendations are made without any guarantee on the part of the author or Publisher, who also disclaim any liability incurred in connection with the use of this data or specific details

We recognize that some words, model names and designations, for example, mentioned herein are the property of the trademark holder. We use them for identification purposes only. This is not an official publication

Motorbooks International books are also available at discounts in bulk quantity for industrial or sales-promotional use. For details write to Special Sales Manager at the Publisher's address

Library of Congress Cataloging-in-Publication Data Available

Lee, John Martin.
    How to restore auto upholstery/ John Martin Lee.
      p. cm.
    Includes bibliographical references and index.
    ISBN 0-87938-948-6
      1. Automobiles--Uphostery--Amateurs's manuals.
    I. Title.
    TL256.L44 1994
    629.26--dc20   94-33834

ISBN 0-87938-948-6

On the front cover: The immaculate tan interior of a Mercedes 300SL. *Dennis Adler*

Printed and bound in the United States of America

Contents

Chapter One

Auto Interior Design

The first automobiles were little more than buggies with engines. As such, seating consisted of a single bench, maybe two, upholstered with button tufted leather.

Like the automobile itself, auto interiors and upholstery have come a long, long way from those first motorized buckboards of a century ago. Autos that were once platforms atop high, thin wire wheels are now low-slung and bubble-shaped, with the front wheels driven by an efficient mechanism a mechanic of 1900 would hardly recognize as an internal combustion engine.

Instead of riding atop this contraption, driver and passenger are now cradled warmly inside in body-embracing bucket seats. Seat belts hold them securely, and an air bag will cushion the blow if their mechanized missile should hit something. At the touch of a button, they can have heat or cool air, stereophonic music, and a digital display to tell how far they have to go and how much fuel they're using.

Button tufted leather upholstery in early horseless carriages like this tiller-steered model was a carryover from the buggy and wagon era.

Modern interiors like this 1993 Eagle Vision are designed and upholstered for comfort and safety. Chrysler Corporation

Buttons and modest stitching are the only decoration of the gray cloth upholstery in this 1936 Oldsmobile.

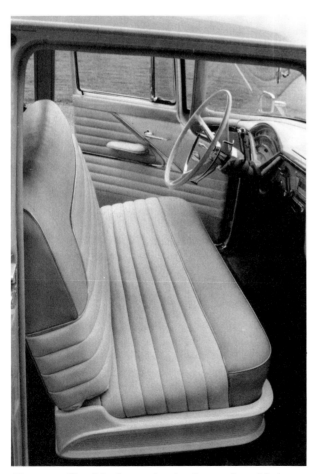

Mercury offered both genuine leather and padded two-tone vinyl as in this 1956 station wagon.

Sports cars like this 1959 Corvette of Keith Petrie popularized bucket seats in the late 1950s.

The Chrysler 300 went the Thunderbird one better by making the front bucket seats swivel for easier entrance and exit.

Fancy 1963 Lincoln Continental provided fold-down center armrests for both front and rear seats.

Nash and, later, AMC Rambler were noted for offering seats that folded into beds. Bob Griffith's 1959 Rambler Cross Country even has screens for the back windows.

Ralph Warnstrom's 1957 Chevy Bel Air Nomad sports a re-stored interior with black jacquard cloth and silver vinyl.

Yes, automobiles went through a multitude of changes. They are an integral part of our collective memory, and that's why so many of us enjoy re-building the older ones we remember so fondly.

Besides an engine and four wheels (usually), the thing one hundred years of automobiles have in common is a place to seat the driver and passen-gers. Interior design has evolved through the years from a buckboard bench to today's plastic and leather capsules. The tasks and materials required to restore the upholstered components depend to a large extent on the era of the vehicle.

In this opening chapter, I'll try to introduce you to some of these interior designs and the up-holstered components and materials you'll face in your restoration project.

Upholstery Materials and Styles

Leather, carried over from carriage and buggy seats, was the upholstery material for the earliest cars. Closed cars were upholstered in woven fab-rics, flat and plain in the cheaper models, padded or tufted in the fancier styles. Luxury cars were of-ten fitted with fancy, high-quality fabrics like bro-cades with elaborate designs, which emulated fur-

niture upholstery of the period.

Upholstery materials and styles were, for the most part, very conservative throughout the thir-ties, forties, and into the fifties. Interiors were not designed to impress or entertain passengers, mere-ly to carry them on plain, bench seats covered in dull grays and tans. Open models continued to be trimmed in leather.

The fifties brought a revolution in automotive styling that also affected the interiors. The flamboy-ant exterior colors and designs were echoed inside. Vinyls that duplicated the look of leather were widely employed. Nylon and rayon ushered in a whole new world of colorful and comfortable upholstery fabrics.

Upholstery materials continued to evolve through the sixties—nylon brocades and vinyl with heat-pressed designs—while interior designs changed.

Luxurious velour fabrics became available to manufacturers in a wide variety of patterns, col-ors, and designs in the seventies. Vinyls also ad-vanced, with new perforated, breathable materials yielding more comfortable seating. Leather began a strong comeback in luxury and sporty models af-ter being shoved aside by vinyl that looked and felt almost as good at a lower price.

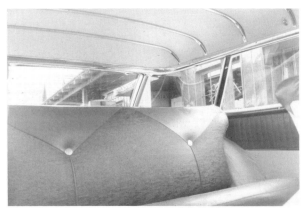

Convertible-simulating chrome bows that first appeared in GM hardtops carried over to decorate the headliners of Nomad station wagons.

Owners jazzed up relatively unattractive package shelves with rolled-and-pleated covers in the sixties.

This full-length console is upholstered, like the seats, in black vinyl with carpeting part way up the sides.

Seating Styles

Individual wraparound seats appeared in the early 1900s; thanks to their water-pail shape they would become known as bucket seats. Some early models had buckets in back. There was even a style with a single bucket seat in the rear known as a mother-in-law seat!

Body-conforming bucket seats evolved through the runabouts and speedsters of the teens, twenties, thirties, and into the post-World War II sports cars. Personal luxury cars of the late fifties and early sixties popularized the style. When Ford upgraded the Thunderbird from a two-passenger sporty car to a four-place luxury cruiser in 1958, the car had bucket seats in front, a back seat padded and upholstered to simulate buckets, and a center console running from the dashboard to the rear. The Chrysler 300, Buick Riviera, and others picked up on this style.

By the mid-sixties every manufacturer offered sporty models with front buckets and center consoles. Headrests were added in the interest of safety, followed by high-back seats with integrated headrests. This arrangement created a barrier between front and rear seat passengers, which became further emphasized when opening rear-quarter windows were replaced with fixed "opera" windows. The rear seat reverted to the more confined compartment of the formal sedans of the twenties and thirties.

Advances in seating technology made seats safer—with built-in headrests and side bolsters to hold the body in position—and more comfortable. A new car buyer can now have seats with ad-

Armrests were integrated into the door panels by the mid-fifties.

The armrest incorporated the door handle and a safety reflector in this 1960 Olds Super 88.

justable lumbar support, not to mention six-way adjustability, at the touch of a button.

Bench Seats

The most common passenger car seating arrangement (until recent years) was the bench seat. Like the carriage seat, the first car seats were literally wooden benches with upholstered cushions for the driver and one or two passengers to sit side by side. If there was a back seat, it was usually the same as the front.

As the industry turned toward closed bodies during the teens, coupes were mainly single-seaters, and sedans had four doors opening to the front and rear seats. Ford, Chevrolet, Dodge, and others built a center door sedan style with a door in the middle of each side for access to both front and back seats.

Two-door sedan and four-passenger coupe styles that developed in the late teens and early twenties had to allow passengers to enter and exit the back seat. On some models, individual front seats pivoted forward on rigid frames, while on others a split backrest folded forward for rear access. The latter is the standard configuration for two-door models today.

Many variations of the bench seat have been introduced over the years. Fold-down center armrests were first incorporated in the more luxurious models. Sometimes the armrest, when flipped up, is the backrest for a center passenger. In 1953, Plymouth split the front seat backrest 2/3–1/3 so passengers could enter the back seat without disturbing a center passenger in front. The 2/3–1/3 or 60/40 split became common in the seventies and eighties. Many contemporary cars have split front seats which can be adjusted independently.

Nash became famous for its optional seats that converted to a double bed. The split backrest reclined so the passenger could nap, or both driver and passenger could pull into a campground and spend the night. In later years, accessory screens for the back windows were offered to provide ventilation while keeping mosquitoes out. In the late fifties, Chrysler pioneered swiveling front seats to make it easier to make a graceful entry or exit. Other makers offered them from time to time as well.

On early station wagons, the cushion of the second seat pivoted forward and the back folded down to make a flat cargo deck. Later designs omitted

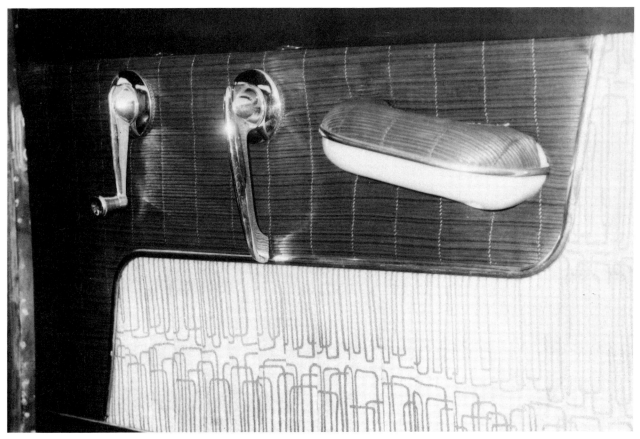

Kaisers in the early 1950s had unique upholstery like the bamboo vinyl and print cloth in this 1953 Golden Dragon.

the first step, leaving the cushion in place and folding the back down on top of it. If there was a third seat, it was removable. Several versions of the fold-down back seat have been adapted to sedans. The latest appear on hatchbacks.

Trim Variations by Series

Just as the higher-priced models of a car line have more bright exterior trim, interiors become more lavish and, in most instances, more comfortable as the price level increases. The popular 1955–57 Chevrolet line is typical. It came in three series. The base One-Fifty series was Spartan, with plain cloth and vinyl trim and rubber floor mats. Two-Tens were upholstered in a better grade of cloth and vinyl than the One-Fifty series. Two-tone vinyl stitched in a rectangle pattern made the Del Ray a sporty, two-door-only addition to the Two-Ten series.

Top-of-the-line Bel Airs were trimmed with patterned cloth, gabardine, and vinyl, and had carpeting instead of rubber mats on the floor. 1956 Bel Air interiors featured Jacquard weave nylon-faced cloth on seats and backrests with leather-grained vinyl in a V-design on seat backs set off by a silver button at the point of each V. Jacquard

cloth and vinyl were combined into a new, more rectangular motif for the 1957 Bel Air models.

Lacking some amenities of its competitors, such as a V-8 engine and a pillar-less hardtop style, Kaiser turned to unusual and fancy trim in its appeal for customer attention. In addition to gold-plated emblems, the 1953 Kaiser Golden Dragon featured unique bamboo-pattern vinyl covering the outside of the top. Seats, door panels, headliner, padded dash, and rear package shelf were upholstered with the same bamboo vinyl and a custom-designed material called Laguna Cloth. The interior and trunk floors were also fully carpeted.

While most cars had standard upholstery, higher-priced, sporty, and limited production models usually had special upholstery. An early example of a distinctive, patterned vinyl appeared in the 1955 Chevy Nomad station wagon. Small, square indentations were pressed into the material, creating a waffle pattern. This waffle pattern vinyl showed up in 1956 and 1957 Corvettes. Thus, demand was sufficient that it has been reproduced.

A drawback for the restorer, however, is that not all of the synthetic "miracle" fabrics of this period were durable. Some were woven with silver and gold threads that snagged; sun, heat, and wear eventually frayed the material. Many special weaves used in low-production cars like the 1956–58 Plymouth Fury have disappeared and aren't being reproduced.

Seat upholstery materials are discussed in more detail in Chapter Three, and sources of materials are covered in Chapter Two. Now let's look at some of the other upholstered pieces of the car.

Carpeting

Next to the seats, the carpeting or floor covering usually gets the most wear. Manufacturers covered the wooden floorboards of early cars with rubber mats. Enclosed interiors protected the upholstery against the weather, and carpeting was installed. Although the materials themselves have progressed, those two floor coverings have been used throughout the years. Carpet is found today in all but the least expensive models. Restorers often prefer carpeted cars because carpet breathes and eventually dries if it gets wet, while rubber mats trap moisture that eventually rusts the floor.

Door Panels

Door panels are highly visible and receive more attention than other upholstered parts (except seats). They hide numerous mechanical components while sealing out noise, dust, heat, and cold. Once plain and utilitarian, they have become highly styled while incorporating door handles and locks, armrests, window and mirror controls, and stereo speakers.

On older cars most door panels are made of upholstery board, a composite material that warps or deteriorates due to age and moisture. Panels on later model cars may have metal or molded plastic components or have a vinyl cover bonded to the composite backing.

Quarter Panels

The quarter panel covers the section between the door and the back seat in a two-door car and between the rear door and the seat on some four-door cars. On a station wagon or sedan delivery the quarter panel extends from the back of the door to the tailgate. The door panel and quarter panel together are also known as the side wall. Side walls are usually designed and upholstered as if they were one continuous panel.

Like the door panels, quarter panels are usually made of upholstery board finished with fabric.

Headlining

The headlining, or headliner, is the inside covering of the roof from the windshield to the rear window and from one side window to the other. Headlining was once tacked to the wooden inner

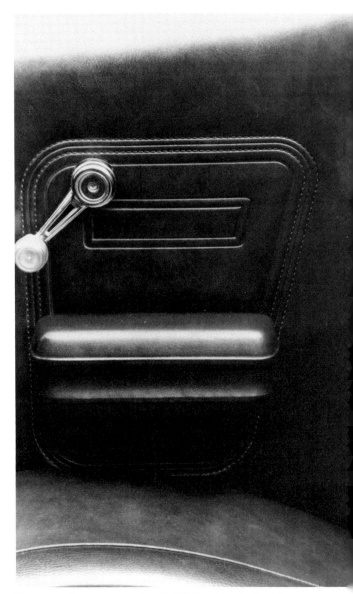

Rear quarter panel in this 1970 Ford Galaxie 500 convertible is covered in smooth vinyl with a stitched design stamped in.

framework of early closed-body cars. After solid steel tops became standard, the headlining fabric was suspended from spring steel rods that followed the top contour and attached at the sides. This type of installation is most likely what you'll be dealing with.

In the sixties, manufacturers began using headliner shells molded to the inside roof contours and made of composition fiberboard material, fiberglass, Styrofoam or a combination such as Styrofoam sandwiched between layers of fiberboard. On economy and utility models, such as station wagons and pickups, the fiberboard may be painted to match the interior color. Manufacturers

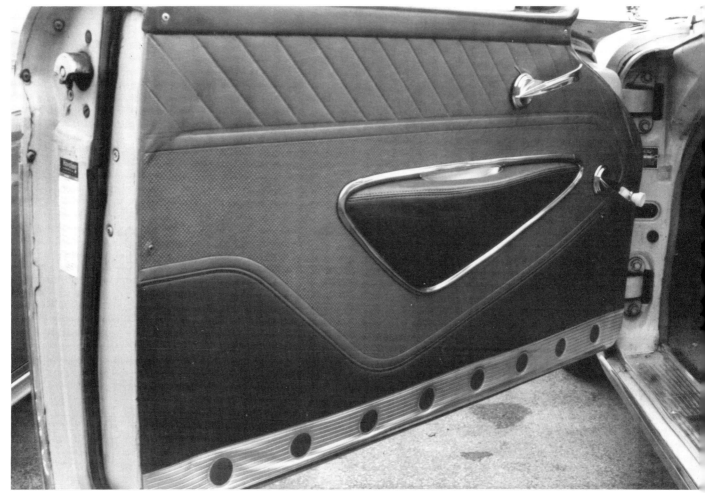

1959 Ford Galaxie door panel is heat-stamped vinyl with a diagonal pleated pattern on top, cross-hatch in the center and darker tone on the bottom with a trim strip of silver Mylar.

finished the headliner panels of some models with foam. Since the late seventies the standard construction has been to cover the shell with foam-backed fabric.

Kick panels

These panels fill the space from the dashboard down to the floor ahead of the front doors. They are usually made of upholstery board and painted or covered with vinyl. Later ones are molded plastic. They hide wires and cables and may contain outside air vents, air conditioner outlets, or stereo speakers.

Package Shelf

The package shelf between the rear seat back and the window is not likely to be upholstered on an earlier model. Made of fiberboard, it is usually just painted, but if strict originality isn't a concern, you may want to cover it with plain vinyl, headlining cloth, or, as later models do, carpeting for a more finished look. Cloth will hide stereo speakers and allow the sound to come through.

Dash and Console

Postwar Chryslers featured a vinyl-covered foam rubber crash pad on the top edge of the dash to help protect front seat passengers in case of an accident. With the flamboyant designs and materials of the fifties, the padded and upholstered dashboard eventually caught on. Later, shock-absorbing pads molded to shape were applied to or incorporated into the dashboard. These are subject to cracking with age and weather. Repair is possible, or the pads can be covered with new vinyl.

The center console came along with bucket seats in the late fifties and early sixties. At first the gearshift lever and perhaps an ashtray and small storage compartment were contained in the console. Tachometers, vacuum gauges, and clocks were added later. Present day consoles may hold drink trays, electric window, and door lock controls, stereo receivers, and tape storage compartments. It's like having an end table with all the necessities beside your favorite living room chair!

13

All or part of the console may be padded and upholstered. The floor carpet often extends to cover the sides of the console.

Sun Visors

At one time, two sun visors helped distinguish a deluxe model. A right side visor was a four or five dollar option on the standard line. Sun visors on both sides have been standard for a long time now. They are usually constructed of a rigid fiberboard material. Sometimes the fiberboard itself is finished, but most often it's padded and covered with fabric to coordinate with the rest of the upholstery.

Armrests

Door panel designs today usually incorporate the armrest with the door handle and window controls. On early cars, if they were included at all, they were attached to the door panel. Later styles are upholstered as part of the door or quarter panel. The earlier style is covered separately and may require some special techniques. Since we grab them to open and close the door and, yes, rest our arms on them, armrests usually need the covering replaced, even if the door panel is okay. Often the padding is damaged, as well.

Convertible Tops

Canvas, vinyl, and synthetic cloth fabric are materials used to make convertible tops. The type you choose will depend upon what the car came with originally, unless you decide to disregard authenticity and take advantage of technological advancements. The top cover attaches to the top framework and to the body at the back of the passenger compartment. Ready-made replacement tops are available for all popular car models in correct materials and colors, but if you have a rare one, it may require making a new top.

Restoring a convertible may also involve replacing the fabric liner of the well the top folds into, the padding over the top framework, the rear window and curtain, and the boot that covers the folded top. All of these components are prefabricated for most models.

As you can see, there are many different upholstered components in a car. A variety of techniques and materials is required to restore them. In the following chapters we'll try to explain and illustrate what you need to know to accomplish the task. If you're lucky, not all of the components on your project will need replacement.

Since convertible tops usually wear out in a few years, ready-to-install replacements are readily available for most models, even this 1948 Lincoln Continental.

Chapter Two

Interior Restoration

Planning Interior Restoration

Time, cost, ability, and necessity are all considerations to be made in planning an interior restoration on your car or truck. First of all, how necessary is restoring the upholstery? If there's nothing but bare springs to sit on, upholstery will be a high priority. On the other hand, the upholstery may be good enough to use while you get the vehicle in shape mechanically and put on a new paint job.

I hope this book will show you how to do your own upholstery restoration and save money in the process, but you must decide how much you can do and the time it will require. The job will probably take you considerably longer than it would an experienced trimmer with plenty of equipment. But if you are restoring a car for fun and a sense of accomplishment and don't have a rigid schedule for doing it, there's no reason not to do it all—including the interior.

Use of the Vehicle

Chances are by the time you're reading this book you've already made the first decision regarding your restoration project: What do you plan to do with it? Will you drive it? Every day, or only for special events and in nice weather? Do you plan to enter it in shows occasionally, or often? If so, how important is winning trophies? Will you get as much enjoyment out of showing just for fun?

Answering these questions will determine how you approach the upholstery as well as every other facet of your restoration project.

I'm always amazed at the insensitivity of a spectators at a car show whose comment to an owner is, "Wow, that's beautiful! What's something like that worth?" Obviously these people know very little about the car hobby. First of all, it's none of their business what someone else's car is worth. It's like asking how much money you make. Secondly, the dollar value of the car is likely of little concern to the owner.

Yes, a restored car is worth more than an unrestored one, but increasing its value is seldom the owner's motivation for restoration. For one thing,

the cost of restoration often exceeds the value of the finished product, especially if much of the work must be farmed out to professionals.

Upholstery for Driving

Recapturing lost youth is the most common reason behind a restoration. Time after time, the owners of cars I photograph say they built the car because it is like one they owned in high school, or it's the one they lusted after but couldn't afford at that age.

Consequently, most people restore old cars to drive, enjoy, and occasionally show. There's nothing like a spin around town or throughout the countryside in a vintage convertible on a sunny weekend! During the summer months there are enough open-air shows, cruise nights, and club outings to fill every weekend in most areas of the country.

Vinyl upholstery as in this 1968 Chevelle wears well and still is easy to clean and keep clean.

Upholstery in this 1956 Chevy is perfectly serviceable for everyday use, but wrinkled seat cushion cover would cost show points. Padding needs to be built up.

If you want to participate in functions like these, a perfectly restored interior isn't necessary. If fact, it may not even be desirable; what if one of the kids spills a chocolate malt on it down at the Sonic Drive-In? That's a good argument for upholstery that's serviceable!

For utility it's hard to beat vinyl, and if your car is from the fifties, sixties, or seventies, chances are that's what it had originally. Even if that's not what your car came with, it looks right for the period. Most custom interiors of the fifties and early sixties were vinyl, so if authenticity is not a prime concern, you may want to consider a period-authentic custom style.

I've also seen many interiors with velour substituted for the original vinyl or hard-to-find woven material in seat inserts. Done in the original pattern, it doesn't look out of place. Chapter Three discusses upholstery fabrics in greater detail.

Authentic Upholstery

If you're thinking of future resale value or are serious about showing or judging, however, nothing but totally correct upholstery will do. Various marque clubs and other show/judging organizations have different standards for judging interior restorations. For your vehicle to judge well in a particular organization, you'll want to restore it according to the rules or guidelines of that organization.

Some are very rigid with regard to redoing the interior only with original materials in original styles. Others may acknowledge that original materials are extremely scarce, if available at all, and impose a lesser penalty on interiors that aren't totally correct.

Club Judging Standards

The Contemporary Historical Vehicle Association (CHVA) covers all makes of vehicles more than twenty-five years old back to 1928. It's impossible for the judging staff to include individuals qualified to discriminate between original and replacement fabrics for every make involved in a show. As long as replacement is of the correct period and type, CHVA judges do not take off points for upholstery, according to CHVA Technical Vice President Dick Benjamin, "unless it is glaringly wrong," such as vinyl in a model that would have originally had broadcloth.

Any deduction for upholstery is discussed with the owner and, if necessary, the chief judge beforehand. CHVA encourages maintaining an original interior or replacement with material exactly duplicating the original and does not knowingly approve the substitution of any incorrect material.

The Kaiser-Frazer Owners Club is fairly lenient in its acceptance of substitute materials. K-F used some unique materials, most of which are not reproduced. K-F club Chief Judge Fred Walker said redone upholstery that is not exactly original but very close is penalized 0.1 point. A 0.2 point penalty is assessed for upholstery that is not reasonably close to original.

Any material "that is original or appears to be original to the official BCA National judging team judging the car" is acceptable to the Buick Club of America. The BCA *Judging Handbook* available to club members includes guidelines for judging point deductions for deviation from standard. BCA judging and awards are based on "how well the car compares to the original factory product," according to 1993 BCA President Bill Bichè.

Classic Chevy International (CCI) judges in both original restored and modified classes. Reupholstering a 1955–57 Chevy with non-original material throws it into the Contemporary Class (one change) unless original replacement material is not available. These models are so popular that several suppliers offer exact reproduction material by the yard or as complete, pre-sewn kits ready for installation. Only interiors for a few of the less popular One-Fifty and Two-Ten models are not reproduced.

Besides authenticity of material and design, CCI judges look for fit, detail, and workmanship. The general appearance of seats and door panels is especially important as a first impression. The CCI *Restoration and Judging Guidelines Manual* available to members contains diagrams and color and fabric charts for every passenger car model from these years plus other excellent information to aid in restoring them correctly.

The Model A Ford Club of America gives full point value to original new old stock and exact replacement upholstery material in its judging. Fabrics used in Model As were common in their day, and these cars were among the first to be targeted by suppliers for reproduction fabric and reupholstery kits, so Model A owners should have no excuse for an incorrect interior.

Accordingly, Model A Club judges routinely deduct 20% to 30% for incorrect replacement material. Other deductions may be made for workmanship and use of non-original upholstery methods.

The International Show Car Association (ISCA) has an antique and restored judging category embracing vehicles that have been returned to as close to original as possible, but there are also "altered" classes which allow up to two changes (for example, upholstery material and wheels.) Changes in more than two areas throw the car into the custom classes. Although they can't always be certain upholstery material is correct, and don't have experts on all makes on hand, ISCA judges look more at whether the material is correct for the period, like the CHVA does, and concentrate on how well the job was done.

The Appendix contains a list of clubs which, while not comprehensive, covers most makes and types of restored vehicles. Joining a national or local club for your make or type of vehicle can be very helpful. You can find out what guidelines they follow in judging, get help locating correct upholstery materials, and maybe even find other members with the same model with whom to correspond.

Scheduling

At what point of the restoration process should you plan to do the interior and upholstery work? It can be done at any time. Generally, it is left until last, sometimes because the restorer is apprehensive about dealing with it and sometimes for more logical reasons: the car is going to be surrounded by dirt, dust and grease as mechanical and body work proceeds; that's not a good environment for new upholstery.

Working on the body will require access to inside panels, floor, firewall, and glass, so upholstered panels, seats and carpet must be removed anyhow. And you surely don't want upholstery in place while the floor, doorjambs, window moldings and dashboard are being painted. There's no guarantee the upholstery can be totally protected even if only the exterior is being painted.

While you don't want to leave new upholstery vulnerable to soiling or damage while doing the rest of the work, there's no reason it can't be done ahead of time and installed only when everything else is finished. You can do upholstery work in the house during the winter, when you don't want to be in the garage wrenching on the engine or sanding the body. Working on upholstery during lulls created by weather or delays in other tasks will help keep the project moving toward completion.

Whether the upholstery is new or you have cleaned and repaired what came out of the car, be sure it is protected until time to install it. Wrap individual parts in plastic or paper and store them in a safe, dry place, along with all the hardware and fasteners that go with them.

There's no set rule for when to do upholstery, but it's important to schedule this phase of the project along with the other work being done. There will be too many variables to determine ahead of time the exact day or even the month, but put the interior work in sequence with the other tasks. Then it need not delay completion when everything else is done and you're eager to get behind the wheel. Planning ahead will also ensure that you have the necessary funds in the budget at the correct time.

Researching Original Designs and Materials

Another good reason for scheduling upholstery work is to be sure you have your homework done.

If the project is missing some or all, the original upholstery, you may have to do some research to find out what it's supposed to look like.

I once photographed a '53 DeSoto convertible the owner had restored from a relic he pulled out of a salvage yard. After years of weathering, there was no top and no upholstery material left. The owner wasn't able to find out what the original material and design had been, so he had a trim shop make up the interior as it might have been in that period. Although it looked great, it was not authentic. If the owner had known where to look, the information was probably available. Where could he have turned to learn how to reproduce the interior correctly?

Clubs and Associations

One of the best sources of information is a club or association devoted to a particular make of car. Clubs and owners associations exist for nearly every make of automobile and light truck. In the case of the DeSoto, there are at last three national organizations: the DeSoto Club of America; the WPC Club, Inc. (Chrysler Products); and the Chrysler Products Owners Club. All have publications that zero in on a particular make or model, and upholstery colors and materials are often covered in detail.

It happens that the *WPC News* issue on the 1953 DeSoto didn't cover convertible upholstery or even offer a photo of a convertible interior, although the 1954 issue did. The description of "bright, gay nylon fabric and rich, genuine leather" indicates that the vinyl in the 1953 model mentioned is probably not right.

Most clubs have members with titles such as "technical advisor" who specialize in specific makes and models. By joining the club (usually $20 to $30 a year), a member can find a knowledgeable resource person for his make and model. Presumably, this person owns or has restored that particular model or has at least collected factory literature, articles, photos, manuals, and maybe dealer showroom albums. If you're really lucky, he'll have a dealer's upholstery sample book from which to select the correct, or desired, material and colors.

Free classified advertising in the club magazine is a privilege of membership in most national clubs. You can use it to publish a notice asking for the information you need. Many clubs also publish a roster of members and the cars they own, from which you may be able to locate the owner of an identical or similar model to help you authenticate your upholstery job.

If members demonstrate sufficient demand, clubs often reproduce needed parts. For example, the Kaiser-Frazer Owners Club has a manufacturing fund that has reproduced excellent rubberized vinyl floor mats and ribbed carpeting.

The Appendix in the back of this book lists the principal national clubs and associations. *Old Cars News and Marketplace* annually publishes a fairly comprehensive list of clubs, as do other hobby publications.

Shows and Meets

Another possibility is to attend the club's national or regional meet, where you might find a correctly done example of the upholstery job you're trying to duplicate, or one of the above-mentioned individuals with information.

The club national meet is also a good place to look for literature on your car. Sales brochures usually show color interior photos and descriptions of upholstery materials. Owner's manuals often have interior shots, too. Literature vendors can also be found at large swap meets and shows, or through ads in hobby publications. Investing in a good color brochure on your car will be money well spent; it can help identify components and their placement.

Magazines and Books

Motor Trend has specialized in testing and evaluating new cars since the fifties. *Hot Rod* also covered many of the performance models. The articles in both of these magazines have been cataloged in the *Reader's Guide to Periodical Literature* since 1959, and larger libraries started their collections of those titles about that time. Check under the heading of "Automobiles" or "Automobiles—Testing" to find what magazines carried articles on your car. *Road & Track, Car and Driver, Popular Mechanics,* and other magazines that may have carried road tests and evaluations of your car may be available at the library, too.

Look for ads in the above as well as in general interest magazines. *National Geographic*, for example, often carried color automobile ads with interior views.

Current magazines on the old car hobby, such as *Special Interest Autos* and *Cars and Parts* have covered hundreds of individual models over the years with detailed photography and descriptions. Contact them to see if they have a back issue featuring your car or one like it.

Look in classified ad publications like *Hemmings Motor News, Old Cars Weekly,* and *Cars & Parts* for literature vendors. Contact them for sales literature and photographs that show the original upholstery for your model.

Studying an unrestored or correctly restored example at a show is the best way to check details of original upholstery, but that's not always possible—particularly for a rare model. Next best would be to find good photos of original or restored examples.

Velour is more comfortable than vinyl to ride on. This owner has substituted diamond-stitched velour for the original material in an otherwise stock 1964 Impala.

Trim codes

Your car should have a paint and trim code on a plate on the firewall. These numbers tell what color of paint and what upholstery was installed at the factory. Information on deciphering trim codes can be obtained from marque clubs, publications, and specialty books like *Last Onslaught on Detroit* by Richard Langworth for Kaiser-Frazer and *The Hot One* by Pat Chappell for the 1955 to 57 Chevy.

The Manufacturer

Auto manufacturers are more interested in how many new cars they sold today and how many they might sell tomorrow than in providing information on one they built twenty or thirty years ago. However, some of them do publish restoration guides containing helpful information, including clubs, parts suppliers, and other valuable contacts.

I contacted the Chevrolet Customer Assistance Center (see Appendix for address), of which the

Club meets like the WPC National for Chrysler products are a good place to see many correctly restored models and visit with their owners.

Special material such as the inserts in this 1960 Oldsmobile Super 88 may not be available. Some judging organizations look only at whether it looks correct for the era.

The trim code on your car's cowl tag tells what the original upholstery colors and materials were.

Chevrolet Hobby Shop is a part, to see what they could provide on the 1946 Chevrolet. They responded with "Past Model Information," a comprehensive list of parts suppliers, clubs, and museums. They also sent another document, "Chevrolet 1946 Specifications," which has complete engineering department specifications for the 1946 models.

In the latter, Fleetline Sportmaster and Aerosedan seat and back cushion upholstery was described as "tan, color-striped 'Fleetweave' flat-woven fabric." The front seat back, side wall, and door upholstery was "tan mixture flat-woven fabric," headlining was "plain tan cloth to match seat upholstery." Sun visors were finished in headlining cloth with brown Spanish grain leatherette binding on the edges. The seat riser and door scuff pads should be finished in brown Spanish grain leatherette to be authentic. Front armrests should have Spanish grain leather on top and door upholstery below, while the rear armrests were upholstered in side wall material. The fiber is not specified on most models, so you can make your own choice if more than one is available (see Chapter Three for a discussion of upholstery fabrics). Bedford Cord (RPO 355) is listed as an option on Fleetmaster sedans and coupes; tan genuine leather (RPO 352) was available in station wagons in place of leatherette.

The document also specifies the type of seats installed in all models and how the upholstery was originally finished. For example, the 1946 Chevy Fleetmaster sport sedan front seat cushion was "plain with French seam at ends;" the back had "thirteen pleats in center, plain ends;" the rear seat cushion was also "plain with French seam in center and at ends;" and the back had "fourteen vertical pleats in center, plain ends." The side wall should have "five horizontal sewed seams just below garnish molding; horizontal bright metal bead at top of scuff pad." Floor covering is listed as "high quality carpet" in Fleetline and Fleetmaster, "good quality carpet" in Stylemaster. Use your judgment.

These specifications are quite explicit and should help a great deal in getting your restoration right. I've seen printed material on later model Chevys (which may also be available from clubs and suppliers) with line drawings of trim designs. All manufacturers may not be able to provide information this complete, but try them. Ask for complete specifications or interior/upholstery specifications for your particular year and model. For "orphans" like Hudson and Packard, try the marque clubs for the same material.

Suppliers

Businesses specializing in parts and supplies for your particular make can be very helpful, especially if they handle the materials you need. Check the list of suppliers in the Appendix and contact those who deal with your type of vehicle. Specify the make, model, year, and body style of your vehicle; include the original color, if known, or the trim code from the cowl tag. Order their catalog to find out what they carry. Some upholstery material suppliers furnish fabric samples to compare with original material. They often have step-by-step installation instructions or photos. If a supplier doesn't have just what you need, they may be able to steer you to another source.

Sources of Materials

An auto trimmer I know was planning to retire after more than forty years in the business. During that time he had accumulated enough upholstery material—leftover roll ends and "generic" material he'd bought in quantity—to fill the two-story house

Kaiser's bamboo vinyl, used both on tops and interiors, is not available. This original material was cleaned up and reused, but the K-F club is fairly lenient in judging.

where his shop was located to the rafters.

I had taken a tour of CARS, Inc., a company in Berkley, Mich., specializing in correct original replacement upholstery for Chevrolets, and knew the owners. To provide ready-to-install kits or yard goods to restorers, they buy original material wherever they can find it, including surplus bought up by wholesalers when production ended. When their stock of a correct, original fabric is depleted, they have it reproduced, usually by the mill that made it originally for Chevrolet.

I contacted CARS about the retiring trimmer. They came, took an inventory of what was in the house and made a deal with the owner to purchase it all. They sorted out the Chevrolet material for their own use and resold the remainder to another firm which handles reupholstery material for other makes.

That's one way restoration upholstery fabric stays in circulation. As mentioned previously, many materials with broad applications have been and are being reproduced. Occasionally, you'll see notices in club publications that a member or the club itself is considering reproducing a particular material, and they want to get an idea of the demand for it. Natu-

rally, having a mill tool up for a run of a particular fabric is expensive, just as it is to reproduce body panels, emblems, weather stripping and other parts. But companies like CARS, LeBaron Bonney and Hampton Coach make a business of it, and everyone in the hobby benefits. The correct materials and installation-ready kits they provide make restoring old cars and trucks a lot easier than it once was.

For example, some acquaintances told of restoring a 1956 Chevy Nomad in the late sixties. Through luck and making a lot of inquiries, they found a trimmer who not only had the obsolete fabric their car required, but expertly crafted it into like-new interior coverings for their Nomad. Hobbyists can accomplish the same job today by ordering a complete interior kit from any of several suppliers and installing it. That is, if they have a 1955–57 Chevy, Model A, Mustang, Barracuda or other popular make.

Owners of many models still have some searching to do. A good place to start is by checking the list of suppliers in the Appendix of this book. Many of the companies sell materials by the yard as well as pre-sewn kits. If they don't have the exact mate-

Modern velour may not be totally authentic, but it looks right for replacing mohair in this prewar Hudson.

rial for a rare model, they can probably come close.

An upholstery shop or fabric supplier that's been in business a long time in your area is also worth checking for obsolete material. And sometimes you have to substitute. You might find a material intended for another purpose that you can substitute for unavailable original material. It's often a matter of luck or persistence in searching through obsolete stocks.

Chevrolet installed vinyl mats under the back seats of 1955–57 Nomad station wagons. Over the years the mats became brittle and broke into pieces. Chevrolet ran off only about 22,000 Nomads, and there aren't enough being restored to justify reproducing the mats. But an alert upholsterer ran across a roll of vinyl-coated boat deck covering made in the sixties that was very close to the texture of the Nomad mat. Cut and fitted to the Nomad rear floor, the mat looks authentic—except for the absence of the Chevrolet part number. With modern dyes the owner can color match it to any Nomad interior scheme.

Your twenties or thirties sedan may have been upholstered with wool mohair, but if you aren't a stickler for strict authenticity, modern nylon velour looks close to the same, is easier to care for, and costs less.

One caution: when shopping for material, remember that some types aren't meant to be used in a car where they're exposed to sunlight and hot and cold temperatures. See a further discussion of upholstery fabrics in the next chapter.

Photograph your Interior

Assuming there is at least some original upholstery in the car now, take a complete set of pictures before you begin. They will come in handy later when you get into installing new upholstery and may have forgotten exactly how a pattern or design was placed. Photographing individual panels will also show you where all the trim and hardware parts are located. As you remove panels, photograph the back sides for trim and clip placement.

Chapter Three

Upholstery Fabrics

When Detroit's auto designers and engineers approach production stage in the development of a new model, specifications for many of the materials and components required to build the vehicle are provided to outside suppliers. These suppliers then prepare proposals to provide quantities of a particular component or product at a specific price.

Textile manufacturers are among the corps of suppliers. The basic specifications they receive for interior fabrics cover such characteristics as weave, fiber content, finish, weight, strength, and color-fastness. Textile suppliers work closely with the automaker's interior designers. The stylists may consider thousands of samples before selecting those they feel are appropriate for their project. The companies then furnish enough material to hand-trim prototypes of the new model. Besides the design staff, engineering and sales personnel usually have input into the final choice of fabrics.

The fabrics are also tested by machines that inflict as much wear in an hour as the material would get in a year in the car. Other machines demonstrate the effects of rubbing against typical clothing fabrics. Further tests determine the tearing points of the fabric, its thread count, and how

much or how little it stretches. The results are compared to the standards set by the trim department.

Once the fabric has received the approval of all concerned and passed the quality tests, the manufacturer will order sufficient quantities to cover their projected production of that model. Thus, the automobile industry and the textile industry jointly determine the look and feel of new car interiors. Materials that perform well and meet consumer acceptance may be continued for several years, with variations in the styles into which they are finished.

Distinctive designs such as the denim blue jean and woven Indian blanket styles introduced by American Motors in the seventies may have a life span of only a year or two in one specific car model. Once that model is discontinued, the pattern is dropped. Unless it becomes popular enough among collectors to justify reproduction, it may be impossible to find an exact match of the original material when restoring a car.

A few colors and designs stay around because car makers continue to order them, or because they are in sufficient demand in the aftermarket or retrimming trade. While the distinctive "waffle" pattern vinyl used in some mid-fifties Chevy and Corvette models and Plymouth's paisley vinyl tops of the late sixties come and go, other vinyl patterns and grains are more or less standard. Demand for certain napped fabrics of the velvet-velour-mohair line or single-color flat weaves may last for years while others may become unavailable a year or two after they were first produced.

When you find the material you need, buy enough for your needs, and don't assume you'll be able to get more two or three years from now.

Auto manufacturers call the shots on interior materials by what they offer to the public. They own the patterns. When the mill fills a manufacturer's order, there's usually an overrun, which the mill retains. When production of a particular model is discontinued, the auto maker will release the surplus. The mill can then sell it to jobbers. That usually takes place about the time the next model

Chevrolet interior designers chose tri-color striped material for the 1958 Impala seat inserts.

is introduced. In other words, when production on 1996 models begins, the 1995 fabrics are released unless the same material is to be continued. If a particular model has sold poorly, the manufacturer may also have leftover quantities of a fabric to offer the jobbers.

Auto upholstery fabric suppliers can buy their goods inexpensively at the time they're released, but they usually have to sit on them for some time. Demand from trimmers for replacement material doesn't build up until a model is at least five years old.

Distributors stock or can get most materials that have appeared in new cars for the past ten years or so. A fabric offered in several models or for several years will be most available because they will have stockpiled it in anticipation of future demand.

Sometimes textile mills will, on their own, produce quantities of a fabric quite similar to the product made for the auto industry and offer it to the aftermarket or retrimming trade.

Fabric History

Leather was used to upholster the earliest cars and is the one material that has survived through the years. It has widespread applications today in upscale models. A by-product of the meat industry, cowhide is the same tough, natural material it was a century ago. Yet, like everything else, leather has changed. Modern methods of processing and dying make it look, feel, and wear better than the earlier product, and it is even more versatile.

Along with closed cars came other types of upholstery materials. Initially, they were adapted from fabrics found in the furniture industry. Later, new fabrics using synthetic fibers were developed especially for automotive applications. These fabrics have almost entirely replaced the natural fiber fabrics in modern cars. In many applications they are satisfactory substitutes for the original, although auto restoration suppliers have many authentic fabrics, too.

Fiber Types

Before discussing fabrics further, we should look briefly at fibers. You may not have a choice of fibers when purchasing replacement material, but if you do, knowing some of the fiber characteristics may be helpful. Many fabrics are blends of two or more fibers—synthetic and natural. Different characteristics make them more or less desirable for automotive applications and may affect how you use them.

Natural Fibers

Natural fibers are derived from plants or animals. Wool and cotton are the most common ones found in auto upholstery fabrics. Linen and silk may appear in furniture upholstery material, but weren't

A car from the twenties may be upholstered in wool.

used much in automobiles. Jute has been employed as backing for carpet, and burlap, produced from jute, is an inexpensive material for covering springs.

Cotton

Restoration suppliers offer 100% cotton headlining in several colors and shades. Otherwise, cotton is not very common. It will be found most often blended with other fibers to produce a fabric superior to pure cotton in most respects.

Cotton's advantages are its ability to retain color and the cool feel resulting from its natural ability to flow air through the weave, or breathe. On the other hand, cotton doesn't wear particularly well and is easily stained and difficult to clean. That's probably why it is used for headlining and not for other parts of the interior.

Wool

The only other natural fiber found in auto upholstery cover material is wool. Genuine mohair, Bedford Cord, and broadcloth are all made of wool, so that's what you'll get if you order authentic replacement material by the yard or a replacement kit. Compared with contemporary nylon fabrics, prices run twice as high or more.

Wool wears very well and is pliable and easy to work with. It is quite comfortable to sit on for extended periods because, like cotton, the fiber breathes.

Synthetic Fibers

Except for the authentic replacement material for the restoration hobby, most upholstery material on the market today is synthetic. It may be all of one fiber, a blend of two or more synthetics, or a synthetic blended with a natural fiber. Often the nap will be of one fiber and the backing of another. Synthetics dominate because they are relatively

Nylon, rayon and other synthetic fabrics were woven into bright, colorful fabrics like the multi-color stripes in this 1961 Plymouth Fury.

inexpensive, exhibit superior strength and long wear, are not subject to bacterial attack and organic decay, and can be produced to closely duplicate the desirable properties of the natural materials.

DuPont started the revolution in the textile industry in 1935 with the introduction of nylon. Much stronger than any of the natural fibers then in use, the new synthetic was inexpensive to produce and could be dyed any color. During the fifties it was combined with cotton and acetate, another synthetic, for an upholstery cloth better and cheaper than pure nylon. Nylon thread eventually replaced weaker cotton thread for stitching.

The synthetics development started by nylon also produced other fibers with characteristics that make them even more appropriate for auto upholstery. Many of the materials on the market are polyesters like DuPont's Dacron. Although rayon's ability to take and hold brilliant color make it useful in blends with high color contrast, other characteristics make it less suitable as an auto upholstery fabric. More and more acrylic has appeared in US mills as they have become more comfortable working with this European-developed synthetic.

Striped body cloth was standard in Dick Yeager's 1937 Ford business coupe.

Nylon velvet or velour substitutes quite well for original mohair at about one-third the cost. Sewn in the original style with buttons and pleats, velour upholstery job looks authentic in Bob Dittrich's 1942 Hudson.

Nylon

The most common synthetic fiber—nylon—can be produced in a wide variety of forms for different uses. Thanks to its versatility, it is found in all types of interior fabrics—velvet/velour, flat cloth, headlining material, and carpeting.

Being very strong, nylon can be made in very fine filaments and woven into a very light and flexible fabric that is still capable of long life. Nylon is also the only fiber that recovers totally to its original shape after stretching. It can be woven with a smooth or a harsh feel, dyed any color, and given a shiny or dull finish. It does, however, retain a sheen that may not be desirable when attempting to duplicate the duller, natural look of cotton or wool.

Nylon's lack of absorbency can be both a bonus and a drawback; it is easily cleaned and dries quickly, but it tends to feel clammy and uncomfortable next to the skin, especially in hot weather. Nylon won't burn, but will melt if it comes into contact with a flame or spark. It also tends to tear easily, yielding to coat zippers and other dull objects. It is not the best material for color retention as it tends to yellow or fade with prolonged exposure to sunlight.

Polyester

Dacron, a product and trade name of DuPont, is the most prevalent of the polyester fibers. It is close to nylon in strength and resistance to wear, although it doesn't stand up as well to extensive weaving. It takes and retains color well and can produce a range of textures from very soft to harsh. Its appearance can range from glossy to dull.

Velvet with a polyester nap is the number one fabric in current Detroit offerings. Polyester may stand alone or be blended with cotton. It is also common as the woven backing for napped fabrics and vinyls.

Acrylics

What nylon has been to the US textile industry, acrylic has been to the European industry—the top-selling upholstery fiber. With most major US mills making it and selling it for the same price as most nylon and polyester, acrylic is making great gains in application. Acrylic is stronger, holds color better when exposed to ultraviolet rays, and is on a par with nylon in wear and durability.

Like nylon, acrylic has a smooth, soft feel. Unlike nylon, it has a somewhat dull finish and can take on the look of wool at substantially less cost. It is most often woven as a pile fabric, or as the surface fabric in a pile weave, and is good for general interior applications.

Rayon

The ability of rayon to take and retain bright colors is offset by its relatively poor strength and durability. Rayon is not found very often in automotive upholstery fabrics except possibly as a blending fiber in fabrics with high color contrast.

Polypropylene

Two of the better-known brand names of this synthetic are Herculon and Olefin. Having very low resistance to the effects of ultraviolet (sun) rays on both fiber strength and colorfastness, these fibers are not suitable for any extensive automotive use. Less expensive than some others, they may appear in blends with other, more ultraviolet-resistant fibers.

Woven Fabrics

Now that we're a little clearer about the characteristics and differences in fibers, let's look further at the woven fabric varieties in which they are used.

Mohair

From the twenties through the forties, when synthetics began taking over, mohair was the most common seat upholstery material in lower- and medium-priced cars. Originally, mohair referred to the hair of the Angora goat, pile woven with a medium-length nap. Eventually the term was applied to any wool cloth with a similar weave. Because of its soft feel and usually gray color, some hobbyists derisively refer to mohair as mouse hair!

Mohair is obtainable, but demand is so small that it's quite expensive. Color selection is restricted to beige, gray, and taupe from some sources, which should be correct for most authentic restorations. But if absolute authenticity is not a concern, modern velvet or velour is a better quality material at about one-third the cost and can hardly be discerned from the original.

Velvet and Velour

By definition, velour is a French name for velvet. The two are essentially the same fabric, so take your choice of which term to use. I use them interchangeably in this book.

Velvet is a thick, short, warp pile fabric, which means the pile (or nap) is woven in the lengthwise direction of the fabric, or along the warp threads, as opposed to the woof, or filler, threads which run across. The most notable characteristic of velvet is its softness. The gowns of fairy tales and couches of royalty were probably made of silk or cotton velvet material. Most modern velvet or velour is made of nylon or a blend of nylon and another thread.

When a piece of velvet is held at the top, the pile will lie down, which is the direction it must be installed. Velvet nap or pile varies in length, or depth, so it's possible to duplicate the original mohair nap.

Crushed velvet is a variation of velvet which has a random, mottled pattern. While material is still hot from the manufacturing process, it is wadded up and put into a large container where it is compressed, literally crushed. The process permanently sets wrinkles into the surface, and the distinctive finish is the result. Crushed velvet was popular for custom upholstery jobs in the sixties and seventies, but I don't remember it being used in a production car.

Once velvet established itself in the seventies as the most popular cloth (as opposed to vinyl or leather) in automobile upholstery material, the fabric manufacturers got really creative with patterns. They wove velvet to resemble Bedford Cord or corduroy ribs, high-low "waffle" patterns reminiscent of Chevy's mid-fifties vinyl on a smaller scale, diamond, tuck-and-roll patterns, and many others. Nylon velvet renders a full spectrum of colors, and many multi-color stripes, herringbone, hound's-tooth, and other designs have been created.

If you're restoring a car from the velvet upholstery era, replacement material should be readily available. When these materials are used to upgrade earlier models, they look (and feel) great even though they aren't authentic. I've seen many beautiful interiors with patterned or plain velvet sewn into the original design. Quilted, tufted or pleated seat and side wall inserts blend nicely with the original-style vinyl. If original woven, brocade, or other special fabric is not available, velvet is a reasonable substitute.

Mid-1970s Cadillac seat wears an example of brocade material.

Body Cloth

Body cloth is a trade term referring primarily to woven fabrics for seat covering. Side walls also may be upholstered with body cloth or with a similar, light weight cloth. Since side wall covering doesn't receive the wear and stress seat covers do, it can be a lighter material.

Body cloth comes in a broad spectrum of colors, finishes, and patterns, including brocades. The main difference in finish is between the napped fabric group, the fuzzy ones, and the flat woven fabrics. Each may be known by other specific terms, including the manufacturer's style name, so don't count on any two trimmers being in total agreement on fabric terminology. Most of today's body cloth is nylon, but suppliers to the restoration trade may offer it in other fibers.

Broadcloth

This is a general term for a number of flat-woven fabrics for upholstering seats, side walls, and trim. Broadcloth is usually wool. It can be dyed any color and woven into various patterns—checks, stripes, herringbone, and even Chrysler's High-lander plaid. Some broadcloths are woven in Bedford Cord or other textures for specific applications.

Bedford Cord

Ford, Chevrolet, and many other makes made extensive use of Bedford Cord upholstery, either standard or optionally. It is a specific variety of broadcloth named for the town in which it was first woven, New Bedford, Massachusetts. It has ribs, or cords, running in one direction. It is smooth, soft, and comfortable.

Antique auto upholstery suppliers listed in the Appendix carry Bedford Cord yardage in correct colors and designs for most of the popular makes, one of which should be suitable even if your car is an uncommon model. The cost is somewhat higher than mohair and comparable to wool broadcloth. Contemporary synthetic velours with a Bedford Cord or corduroy-type weave may be alternatives when the exact original material is unobtainable.

Brocade

Brocade is a flat-woven fabric with a design in the weave that is usually raised slightly from the surrounding surface. A different thread or color may also be used to make the design more distinct. New Yorkers, Caprices, LTDs, and other luxury models came with brocade upholstery. Since many of these patterns were unique to one series of cars and may have been changed each year, they are probably the most difficult to find. Few of them are in sufficient demand to be reproduced. Suppliers who specialize in obsolete fabric may have bought up overruns or leftovers from various sources. If an exact match is not possible, send a sample of the original and have the supplier choose something close.

Headlining

Because it's not subject to much stress or wear, and because it must hang from bows or be glued to the roof insert, headlining is a lightweight material. Cloth headlinings are woven flat or with a short nap, usually in solid, neutral shades.

In the fifties, vinyl came into use for headlining. It added lighter, gayer colors, perforations, and patterns to the finish. Headlining vinyls are lighter weight than those for seats and side walls. Since many different designs were offered, you'll want to find out if a replacement is available before tearing out the one you have. Since vinyl is quite sturdy, it might be possible to clean and reuse it, although seams may need to be restitched and new listing strips installed.

Some suppliers listed in the Appendix make

1955 Nomad "waffle" pattern vinyl was shared later with Corvette.

Headliner material is lighter-weight vinyl or fabric.

Versatile and durable vinyl has been an upholstery mainstay since the 1950s.

headlinings ready to install in many popular makes, which will save you a lot of time and work.

Not all vehicles had upholstered headlining. Pickups, station wagons, sedan deliveries, and inexpensive models used fiberboard inserts painted to coordinate with the upholstery.

Other Fabrics

Many other specific types of weaves and finishes appear in auto upholstery. Some are used for trim, welting, and windlacing. Again, if your vehicle is a fairly common one, trim suppliers will probably have the correct replacement material and can furnish something close to original for hard-to-fit models.

Vinyl

During the synthetic revolution of the fifties, manufacturers touted interior materials with exotic names like Naugahyde and Morrokide. They are brands or varieties of vinyl. The vinyl name applies to a group of chemical compounds derived from ethylene to form plastics and resins. One form of vinyl is the rigid plastic from which dashboards and trim are formed; the soft leather-like materials used for seat coverings is another form.

Although we talk about upholstery material being vinyl, the actual vinyl is the flexible plastic layer on top of a cloth backing. The first product of this type had a coating of a nitrocellulose compound on a coarse woven cotton backing. Developed as a substitute for leather, it was known as "leather-cloth" or "leatherette."

The first leatherette didn't stretch and was subject to cracking, which limited its applications. It was supplanted by vinyl, which first appeared in cars in 1947 as a flexible plastic coating on a cloth backing. In the early fifties, US Rubber Co. (now UniRoyal) introduced its trade-named Naugahyde with the vinyl coating applied to a stretchable knit backing for greater flexibility and broader application. Named for Naugatuck, Connecticut, the location of UniRoyal's plant, Naugahyde became so popular and well-known that it is seldom capitalized anymore and often used generically to apply to any knit-backed vinyl material.

The industry has continued to develop better varieties of vinyl; those available now are far superior to the original materials of the fifties. The main criticism of vinyl seat covering has always been that it doesn't absorb moisture or flow air, so

29

Vinyl can be molded into an infinite variety of grain textures and patterns. Seat inserts in this 1965 Ford Galaxie 500 have very thin horizontal lines and fancy, embossed center stripes.

riders become sweaty and uncomfortable in hot weather. It can also be cold, stiff, and uninviting in very cold weather. In more recent years, breathable vinyls have been developed with thousands of invisible pores which let air pass through and help keep passengers cool. Some vinyl coverings have larger holes as part of the design, which also improves airflow and comfort.

The application of vinyl for auto upholstery began in the fifties and expanded throughout the sixties and seventies. It remains a favorite material, usually found today as the main covering in less expensive models and as trim for cloth and leather coverings. Its serviceability and ease of working and sewing make vinyl ideal for all the little extra spots like kick panels, sun visors, rear package shelves, dashboards, trunk compartments, and covers for folded convertible tops.

Auto interior designers like vinyl because it is relatively inexpensive and can be embossed with an infinite variety of grain patterns. It accepts any color or design and retains its brightness well. Since the coating and, usually, the fabric backing, are synthetic, vinyl is immune to rotting and decay. If your project car is upholstered in vinyl, try cleaning and treating it with a good conditioner

and see how nice it looks. You might get by without replacing it. I've seen restored cars still wearing the original twenty-five-year-old vinyl.

Leather

The one upholstery material that has always been around and probably always will be is leather. Carriage and buggy seats were upholstered in leather long before cars were invented. Its popularity may rise and fall, but the quality and luxury of leather remain constant.

Many of the finest cars throughout automotive history have been upholstered in leather. Since it has superior strength and is long-wearing, limousines and town cars often used leather for the chauffeur's compartment, while the wealthy owner rode in back on soft brocade cloth. In the classic era some top-of-the-line car interiors had leather everywhere, even underneath the cowl and as binding on the carpet. Now its most common application is on the wear surfaces of the seats. Good leather is fairly easy to work with and can be sewn into any style and pattern.

But good leather does not come cheaply. Don't jump into reupholstering a leather interior until you're certain the leather in your car cannot be sal-

30

vaged. Companies such as Color-Plus (listed in the Appendix) make products to condition, resurface, and recolor old leather so it looks new again.

Leather Processing

One reason vinyl was developed was to approximate the look, feel, and wear of leather at a fraction of the cost. The supply of leather is not a problem; as a by-product of the meat industry, plenty of the raw product is available. The expense comes in the long, involved process of turning raw cowhide into usable leather upholstery material.

Nearly all the leather for automotive upholstery is cowhide, although some buffalo hide is used. The hides of pigs, goats, horses, deer, and other animals are also tanned and made into leather, but mostly for clothing and other applica-

tions. The series of operations begins with washing the hide, removing the flesh and hair, and then scrubbing it in chemicals to remove any remaining animal protein and agents used in the hair removal process. Finally the hide is "pickled," or washed in a weak acid solution in preparation for tanning.

The tanning process converts the hides into a stable, durable material with a long service life. Chrome sulfate is the tanning agent in the modern, two-stage process resulting in a uniform, durable product.

After tanning, the hide proceeds through the currying process of soaking, splitting, dressing, and coloring. The splitting procedure is literally a slicing of the hide by a special machine to yield a material of uniform thickness. Thus, top grain

Black leather is featured along with a work table in George Boellert's 1967 Imperial Director's Coupe.

31

leather or cowhide refers to the top layer of the hide. Thicker top grain leather goes into auto upholstery while the thinner leathers are used for furniture and wearing apparel, where a lighter, softer material is desired.

The other layers, called "split grain" or "flesh splits," are resurfaced and can be embossed to resemble the original surface pattern or imitate the grain pattern of other animals.

After being tanned and dried, the leather is dry and stiff. A process called "fatliquoring" flexes and softens it with oils, adding strength to the fibers and maintaining pliability so it can be stretched and dried without again becoming stiff and unmanageable. If the surface needs to be smoothed, it is sanded or buffed. The highest-quality leather requires no buffing and is called "full top grain."

The most thorough coloring method is vat dying, which originally meant soaking the entire hide in a colored dye. Now it may be run through a series of rollers which apply the dye. A vat dyed hide will have uniform color all the way through, which helps to hide minor cracks and abrasions. The process is rather expensive and seldom done for automotive leather.

A hide with color on the outside and natural (tan) on the inside has had the color sprayed on. Since colors used in vat dying are somewhat limited, these hides are usually surface coated, as well. Earlier leather finishes of nitrocellulose lacquer became brittle and cracked or rubbed off over time. European leathers are still produced with nitrocellulose lacquer coatings. In this country, leather and vinyl coatings are polymer-based. They never become stiff and brittle and wear extremely well. Coatings are sprayed on or applied by mechanical rotating brushes in seasoning machines.

Surface coloring follows the final buffing step. Often the leather surface is embossed with a grain pattern at this time, too. A protective top finish coat applied over the color prevents the color from rubbing off on clothes and resists staining and cracking.

Choosing Leather

American cattle spend most of their lives contending with the elements on the open range. Consequently, they develop thick hides. European cows, on the other hand, are pampered and sheltered in barns, so their hides tend to be finer, thinner, and

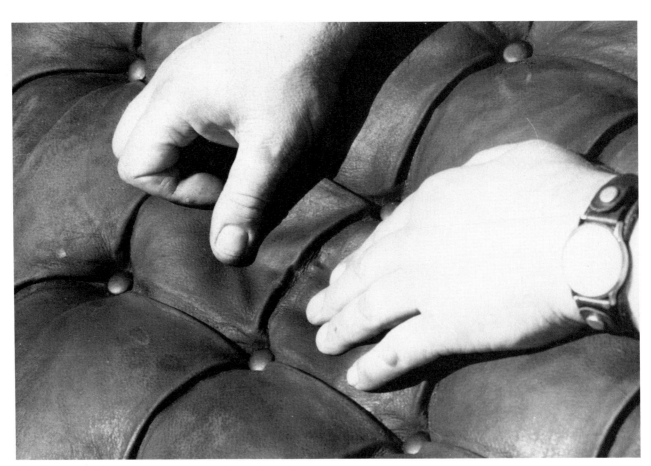

The leather on this antique car seat is dry and weather-checked, but still holding together after more than 70 years.

unblemished. American leather is tougher, but is likely to have scars caused by barbed wire, brush and shrubs, and insect bites. European leather is fine in quality, but not as durable.

A car owner or manufacturer may boast of his or her Connolly leather upholstery, and with justification. Connolly Brothers of London is not only the world's largest supplier of upholstery leather, they are also one of the oldest, having been in business for well over one hundred years. Connolly has a reputation for producing high-quality hides with uniform color, finish, and texture. Prices for Connolly leather depend upon exchange rates, but because of its volume, the company is often competitive with US suppliers.

When shopping for leather, look for the company's brand name stamped on the back side of the hide. Reputable suppliers from every country maintain a certain standard of quality and are proud to identify their products. Stay away from unbranded hides. Some cut-rate suppliers shortcut the tanning processes to market a product inferior in flexibility and uniformity, resistance to staining and cracking, and colorfastness.

If you have the opportunity to choose your own leather, inspect it carefully for small holes and scratches. Near the edge of the hide these imperfections may not bother, but if they're in the middle, cutting around them can waste too much material. Check the hides for uniformity of grain, color, and thickness. If there is variation, be sure there are sufficient expanses of the thicker material to cover the seats, where stress is greater. Smaller, thinner pieces can be used where they won't be stressed or their unevenness won't be so noticeable.

Unlike materials manufactured or woven in uniform widths, rolled, and sold by the yard, leather is sold by the hide or half hide and priced by the square foot. Hides are just as they come from the cow, which means irregularly shaped and variable in size. An average-size full hide will be around forty-five square feet. The range is from thirty-two to fifty-five square feet.

For estimating purposes, one or two hides should cover the seating surfaces of a pair of low-back bucket seats, and two or three should do the seats and cockpit of a two-place roadster. To cover the front and rear seats of a full-size hardtop or sedan will require four to seven full hides, more if the design involves a lot of pleating or tufting. Notice, however, how much of the original upholstery is leather. Many models, especially from the sixties on, used leather only for seat inserts and matching vinyl for bolsters, trim and side walls.

Finally, before tackling a leather interior job, get plenty of practice on vinyl or some scrap material of similar texture. Leather is simply too expensive to experiment on, and every stitch

hole in the material is there for good. There's no going back to repair a cobbled job.

Carpeting

Carpet material is a woven fabric manufactured in a similar way to those we've been discussing. Besides a floor covering, it has often been applied to the lower edges of door and quarter panels and, sometimes, to seat bolsters.

As with other upholstery fabric, carpeting has specific characteristics when made for automotive applications, since it must withstand exposure to extremes of heat and cold, certain wear patterns, and moisture.

Carpet fiber changed over the years, from 100% wool to various rayon and nylon blends in the fifties and sixties to polyester and 100% nylon. Since the early seventies, most original equipment carpet has been a rayon/nylon blend or 100% nylon. Chances are good you can find the correct material for your vehicle, or you might choose a contemporary synthetic fiber that looks correct. Several of the suppliers listed in the Appendix offer carpet material and/or carpet that is pre-cut and sewn or molded to the floor pan contours of specific models.

If the supplier offers carpet that correctly duplicates the original, fine. If not, the other characteristic to consider is the pile, or nap, of the carpet. The wool carpet in many cars of the thirties and forties was woven with a short pile that gave it a velvet look. The pile consists of threads or yarn woven in loops and bonded to a woven backing. Carpet left this way is known as "loop pile." The depth of the loop pile may vary from nearly flat to deep. In some instances the loops are formed into rows to create a ribbed pattern, but most of the time they are random so the surface is uniform. Different styles of loop pile with names like Tuxedo Loop (also known as salt and pepper) and Daytona Loop were used in some fifties and sixties models.

To create cut pile carpeting, the ends of the loops are shaved off, leaving the fibers sticking up like bristles on a brush. Sometimes it is made by weaving the pile threads through two layers of backing with space between, then slicing through the space to create the cut pile. Again, the pile may be short or deep, depending upon the depth of the loops to begin with. It seems carpet pile has gotten deeper and more plush as automakers have built more luxury into their offerings, but most work on older cars will be with the shorter varieties. With luck you will be able to salvage at least a scrap of the original carpet to determine a correct match. If the carpet supplier can't match it, you may need to do further research or contact the owner of a similar vehicle for help.

Some cars also used carpet in the trunk, while others used mats. Reproductions of either are available for most popular models.

Chapter Four

Cleaning and Repairing Upholstery

The interior of your newly-acquired project car or truck may look like a shambles, but before you dive in and rip out all the upholstery and throw it away, take a little time to clean it up. You could find it's not so bad once years of soil and neglect are removed.

Unbolt the seats and get them out where you can brush and vacuum them, then see what condition they're in. If there's leather, that's very expensive. Try to save all you can. Even if the fabric is shot, don't be quick to get rid of it.

Getting the seats out affords you a good look at the carpet, side panels, headliner, and miscellaneous other pieces. The carpet may be serviceable with a good cleaning, but you might leave it in while you work inside; it's easy on the hands and knees and can catch fasteners you drop. Whether you remove the side panels for cleaning is a matter of convenience.

In this chapter, we'll take you through several cleaning and repair procedures that might help you save at least some of the interior trim. At any rate, don't throw anything away just yet. You might need it for a pattern or to match new material.

Fabric Cleaning and Repair

A workbench or picnic table is a good place to give seats a thorough cleaning. Whether you remove door panels and other panels will depend upon how complicated the process is and how much work they need.

Start by vacuuming to remove loose material, especially in pleats and tufts where dirt collects. Try to identify and remove visible stains before shampooing the entire seat or panel. If stains have been there for a long time, however, you may not be able to identify them, let alone budge them. The best approach would be to mix up fabric shampoo as described a little later and pre-treat the stains, scrubbing with a rag or brush before you shampoo the entire piece.

Here are recommended treatments for some common stains if you can catch them when they're fresh:

Blood: cold water, a little household ammonia if water doesn't get it all;

Chewing gum: scrape off as much as possible, remove the residue with naphtha, kerosene or lighter fluid;

Chocolate: warm water followed by carbon tetrachloride or similar cleaner;

Grease and food: Energine or soap and warm water;

Paint and shoe polish: turpentine, but avoid paint remover or brush cleaner;

Tar and road oil: turpentine or lighter fluid.

But don't stop with just scrubbing out stains or soiled areas. Chances are the upholstery has faded so the cleaned spot will stand out like a beacon. After working the stains, clean the whole panel or seat.

Is the upholstery over foam padding, on the seats, for example? If so, avoid soaking; the padding is slow to dry. Never use mineral spirit solvents or strong chlorine solutions on fabric covering foam rubber, either.

A dry foam cleaner or a commercial upholstery shampoo that makes a thick, soapless lather is recommended for such an application; follow the directions. Various upholstery cleaning products are specially formulated for certain fabrics such as velvet or velour.

Woolite and a little cold water works well on wool, mohair, and synthetic fabrics. An upholstery shampoo can be made by dissolving six tablespoons of pure, white soap flakes in a pint of boiling water and adding two tablespoons of ammonia or two tablespoons of borax as a softener. Let the mixture stand until jelled, then whip it into a lather. The lather, without water, does the cleaning; the fabric should absorb as little moisture as possible.

Apply the shampoo to seat or side panel upholstery with a soft brush, working on no more than a square-foot area at a time. Wipe it off with a clean cloth or sponge wrung out of clean, warm water, and allow it to dry out of direct sunlight. Fabric with a deeper nap may need to be vacuumed again after it dries. Spraying fabric with a protectant such as Scotchgard will help it resist future spills and stains.

Pristine interior of a 1971 Dodge Challenger.

Take seats out and put them on a table or other surface where you can work on them easily.

Cleaning Vinyl

Two types of vinyl material are found in auto interiors—flexible vinyl for seat covers and side panels and sometimes headliners, dash covers, and other parts; and rigid vinyl for dashboard pads and interior trim pieces. Generally, vinyl is not harmed by common chemicals and resists acids, alcohol, and stains, but avoid using harsh chemicals like ammonia, lacquer thinner, acetone, or abrasives to clean vinyl parts.

Vacuum upholstered pieces first. When well maintained, vinyl requires only wiping with a damp cloth. If it is badly soiled, hand wash it with warm water and soap or synthetic detergent. Sponge a good-sized area and allow the solution to remain for a minute or two, then rinse with a damp sponge. A soft-bristle brush may help on stubborn spots.

Opinions are divided on using protectants on

After cleaning vinyl with soap and water, some car owners and auto detailers recommend a protectant to keep the material soft and pliable.

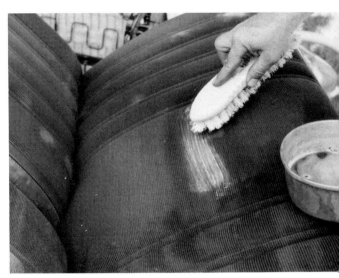

Treat spots and stains on the fabric first.

These Mustang seat covers are in pretty bad shape, but the desirable "pony" inserts could be salvaged and sewn into new covers.

vinyl. Manufacturers recommend their products to keep vinyl soft and pliable and make it easier to keep clean. However, I've heard claims of chemical protectants, combined with heat and sun, discoloring the material. To be safe, conduct your own experiment on some scrap vinyl first.

Saddle soap can keep vinyl soft and shiny without the problems some chemicals might cause. Rub it on with a damp cloth and buff it when dry. Saddle soap also renews rubber parts like weather-stripping and window seals.

Cleaning Leather

As with other materials, begin leather cleaning with the vacuum cleaner to remove loose dirt, but use a brush attachment to avoid scratching the leather. Wash with warm, soapy water. Wet a soft cloth and wring out most of the water to avoid soaking the leather. If the leather is especially soiled, spray cleaners can be used with a damp cloth. Spray the cloth rather than directly onto the leather, and rinse the cloth often in clean, warm water. A soft bristle brush will help remove soil from creases in the leather surface.

Rinse well with a cloth wrung out of clean, warm water. Any cleaning agent left on the surface will attract dirt. Allow the leather to dry thoroughly before using or conditioning it.

Leather will dry out and gradually lose its natural oils with use. Periodically applying a conditioner will keep it supple. Soffener Leather Conditioner by Color-Plus, a high concentration of actual animal oils, is one such product. Apply it first to seams or other spots where the leather has been punctured, thus providing an opportunity for the release of oils; then apply a light coat to the entire surface. Allow several hours for the conditioner to penetrate thoroughly. Follow by buffing off any excess with a clean, soft, dry cloth.

Refinishing Leather and Vinyl

Refinishing leather and vinyl with the Color-Plus process and products is said to be similar to refinishing furniture. You may be able to avoid the expense of replacing worn leather and vinyl upholstery, or change the color. There are numerous other dyeing or recoloring products, but be sure to get a reputable one. Some products promoted as leather and vinyl dye are no more than paint that will crack, peel, or rub off with use. They look fine, however, in places subject to little flexing or rubbing.

Directions for Color-Plus' process call for removing the color coating of leather with paint remover, using sandpaper on stubborn spots. Vinyl is cleaned thoroughly. Either surface is then prepared by sanding with fine grit sandpaper.

If there are deep cracks in the leather or vinyl surface, Color-Plus has a flexible filler to fill them. Then the area is sanded smooth. If leather is split

Vinyl seat covers commonly split where pleats are pressed or sewn in. This kind of damage is virtually impossible to repair, especially with the stress a seat cover is subjected to.

or nearly so, the area can be reinforced by gluing a piece of leather or canvas to the back with contact cement. If the back side isn't accessible, it is possible to slip the reinforcing piece through the slit, glue one side and then, after it dries, work cement beneath the other side. Once the repair is made, the resulting scar can be filled as above. Sometimes several coats of filler are required to build up the surface.

Color-Plus recommends their own Soffener Leather Conditioner to restore the oils that make leather soft and supple. Vinyl cannot be re-softened once the plasticizers in it migrate into the at-

This vinyl seat cover has split at the seam. It can be repaired, but to do it right the cover should be removed and the seam resewn.

mosphere. But vinyl usually remains supple for a long time, and as long as it is, you can refinish or recolor it with the same procedure as for leather.

Surflex Flexible Surface Colorant can be applied with a soft-bristle brush or with a spray gun. Try it out on a scrap or an inconspicuous area to get the feel for the application technique and coverage. Then apply a thin coat to the entire surface and, after it's dry, follow up with subsequent light coats to achieve an even finish. The surface colorant dries for use in a day. After curing for about six weeks, the recolored leather or vinyl can be cleaned and cared for just as the original material.

The ability to recolor these materials also raises the possibility of swapping in a seat or panel with better upholstery and recoloring it to match the interior. Replacing worn or torn sections or changing the entire interior color scheme are other options. Of course, if the original upholstery is so faded a recolored piece won't match, you may end up doing both seats or the whole interior anyhow.

Regular cleaning and treatment with one of the products previously mentioned or saddle soap, neat's-foot oil, or lanolin will keep leather and vinyl upholstery soft, supple, and attractive. Protect leather from excess sunlight and moisture. The former will dry and fade it, the latter can cause an organic material like leather to rot. Leave vents open and a window down a crack to provide ventilation while the car is in storage. Protect it with a breathable fabric cover.

Upholstery Repairs

Inspection of a damaged panel or seat should provide a good idea of whether it can be repaired and how much work it would involve. Often the seam threads wear out and let go while the surrounding material is still good. Resewing the seam may seem to be a simple task, but not if you have to remove the entire seat cover to do it. If there's a way to clamp the joining pieces together, you can often restitch a seam by hand with a curved needle that allows you to work from the outside.

Even taking off the cover and restitching any loosened seams by hand may save time and expense over new upholstery. Knot any loose or broken thread so it won't unravel further. In some instances you may be better off to take out a whole seam and resew it on a machine.

It's not uncommon for fabric covering to pull loose from side panels. Remove the panel and make sure the trouble isn't caused by a warped or rotted panel board. You can glue a new piece of panel board to the back of the first to reinforce it. If a section is rotted away, pull the fabric out of the way, and use a straightedge to cut back to solid panel material on a straight line. Cut a new piece of panel board and butt-join it to the original with duct tape on both sides of the seam. Coat the panel with waterproof material such as Thompson Water Seal or Weldwood Woodlife to prevent future damage.

Scrape off old cement, spread new cement on both the panel and the fabric edge and when it becomes tacky, stretch the fabric over and press it down firmly. Staple around the edge to help prevent the fabric pulling loose again. Before reinstalling the panel, be sure drain holes in the door or body are clear to avoid future moisture build-up.

Repairing Cloth Upholstery

When cloth upholstery wears to the point that the weave is separating, there's often little recourse but to replace it. A single cut or tear, however, might be repaired as we described earlier, by pulling the edges together and gluing or sewing a patch underneath. Invisible in-weaving has saved many a cigarette-burned dress or suit, and the same technique can be used on upholstery fabric. Sewing shops, dry cleaners, and (sometimes) used car dealers may refer you to someone with this skill.

Vacuum the carpet to remove loose materials.

Fancy fabrics, especially some installed in the fifties, often fell apart while the surrounding vinyl trim remained intact. You may be able to take seat or side panel covers apart at the seams and sew in new inserts, if the correct fabric or an acceptable substitute can be found.

Cleaning and Renewing Carpets

The best job of cleaning the carpet can be done out of the car. On modern cars that usually entails removing the door sill plates and pulling the carpet out from underneath side and firewall panels. If carpet is glued down, you can clean it in the car by hand or use steam to loosen the glue and a putty knife to work it loose. Very early cars may have metal fasteners which hold the carpet to the wooden floor.

Shake the carpet well, or hang it up and beat it to remove loose dirt and dust. Then place it on a flat surface and follow up with a vacuum cleaner. Shampoo the carpet with a commercial product or your own sudsy solution of detergent and water. Scrub the carpet by hand with a stiff brush or, if it's convenient, with a power carpet shampooer. Rinse with clear water and allow the carpet to dry.

Most shampoo products recommend vacuuming again after the carpet is dry. Be sure to shake or beat dirt out of the padding or under layer, also.

If your carpet isn't presentable after a thorough cleaning, you're probably due for new carpeting. The only alternative might be if a worn or damaged section can be cut out and a new, matching piece fitted. Sew or tape it into the hole if the carpet is loose, or glue it to the floor. Hiding the repair may be a trick, but plush or cut pile should blend in quite easily.

Spray-on fabric dyes that can renew your carpet's color are available. This is best done with the carpet out of the car. Be sure to clean it thoroughly and follow the dye manufacturer's directions.

To help keep new or renewed carpet nice, you can make removable mats by sewing binding around the edges of surplus carpet pieces for use in high-wear areas.

Other Interior Components

While the seats and carpet are drying, turn your attention to other matters. In cleaning upholstered side panels, door panels, and the dash, an old toothbrush will reach into cracks, and a rag or

Door sill moldings hold the carpet edges in most modern cars. Sometimes a rap of the hammer on the Phillips screwdriver helps jar the screw loose.

towel folded over a table knife will also get into tight spots in vinyl and hard parts. Use Q-tips to clean out cracks and mounting screw holes and to wipe out water that drips into cracks. It's not upholstery, but tar stains inside ashtrays can be dissolved with toilet bowl cleaner.

Clean the seat belts with soapy water and a brush, then rinse and hang them up to dry. I once wanted to change a set of light brown belts to dark brown to match some new upholstery I'd installed. The RIT dye people wouldn't endorse using their product because the web belts are so tightly woven, but I tried it anyway. Following directions on the box, I heated the dye in a large, old cooking pot and soaked the belts until they took on a dark, even tone, then rinsed them and let them dry. It worked fine, and there was never a problem with the dye rubbing off on clothes.

Scrub the pedals with a stiff brush and pick bits of gravel out of the cracks with an awl or a small screwdriver. Apply a dressing to give them a new appearance. Metal parts can be wiped clean with a damp cloth or washed with soap and water, if necessary. Wash the door sills underneath the sill plates and all around the door jambs. Shine up the painted parts with liquid or paste wax and chrome and stainless with chrome polish. Don't, however, use it on chrome-plated plastic parts. Their finish is not tough like chromed metal and can be easily scratched or rubbed off. Use soapy water and a soft cloth on these pieces. Here's a tip: if the bright finish on an armrest mount is damaged or worn, it possibly can be turned upside down or swapped to the other side to put the worn area out of sight.

Vinyl and Convertible Tops

Regular washing will help keep a vinyl or convertible top in good condition and avoid the build-up of grime and stains that is difficult to remove. Always wash the top in shade. Carefully vacuum a fabric convertible top to remove excess dirt and foreign particles before washing. Wet the entire car. Apply a mild liquid soap solution with a washing glove or sponge. Stubborn stains may be removed with Rhinyl Coat cleaner or Meguiar's Mirror Glaze 39 and a soft-bristled nylon brush. Be sure to rinse away all traces of soap or cleaner.

Removed from the car and spread out on a clean surface, the carpet can be shampooed with a household machine.

Rhinyl Products recommends their Rhinyl Protective Treatment or Meguiar's Mirror Glaze 40 as a dressing to extend the life and good looks of a vinyl top. There are other dressings and preservatives, but be sure you know how they work, or test them first.

Small rips and tears in vinyl tops can be repaired with a dab of clear nail polish, or a small patch of matching vinyl can be applied with adhesive. Tears in cloth convertible tops can sometimes be repaired satisfactorily by either sewing the separation shut or sewing a patch to the under side.

Dust and dirt or other harsh material will scratch a convertible's plastic rear curtain. When cleaning, place the car in the shade, wet the surface thoroughly and do a minimum of rubbing with a soft cloth. Do not dry by rubbing; pat dry with a soft cloth or chamois. Use Meguiar's Mirror Glaze Plastic Cleaner and Plastic Polish or a similar product to restore clarity and extend plastic window life.

Now that the car's interior is clean, you can make a better assessment of what repairs and replacements will be required to restore it.

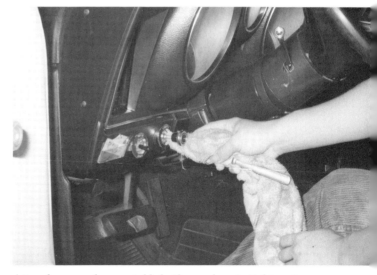

A towel wrapped over a table knife can clean in tight spots.

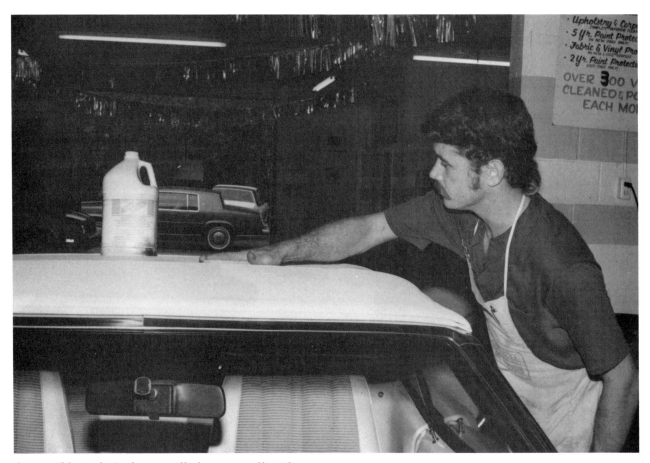

Convertible and vinyl tops will clean up well with a good scrubbing with a good quality cleaner and treated for longer life.

Soak and scrub the rubber pedals while they're out of the car.

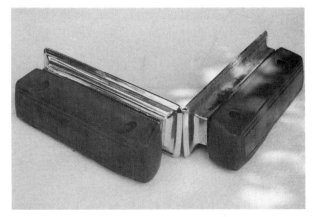

The Dodge chrome-plated plastic armrest base on the right was turned over to hide the worn finish, leaving the visible top surface looking new as on the left.

Use an old toothbrush to clean in cracks and around hardware.

Chapter Five

Supplies and Tools

By now you probably have the upholstery fabric to recover your car's interior, or you've at least made a selection and know where to get it. But many other important materials are involved in reupholstering a car. The padding determines how comfortable the seats are and how well they last. Door and side panels won't look their best or last as long as they should if the panel material and the adhesive or fasteners attaching the upholstery to it are of poor quality.

In this chapter we'll look at these other necessary items and the tools required to do a quality upholstery job.

Upholstery Material Suppliers

Upholstery supply firms are found mainly in larger cities. More of them specialize in furniture upholstery than in automotive upholstery, although many supplies apply to both. Also, they are often wholesale firms, dealing only with established trim shops, not with individuals. You may be able to work through a local trimmer to obtain the necessary special supplies.

Many of the suppliers listed in the Appendix handle full or partial lines of upholstery and interior supplies. LeBaron Bonney, for example, began manufacturing complete upholstery kits for early Fords in 1960. Now, in addition to kits for Fords and Mercurys from Model A through the early fifties, they also carry reproduction seat frames and springs, convertible top bows and frames, floorboards and mats, door handles and window cranks, hundreds of hardware items, and more, to make redoing one of these models a snap.

Firms offering reupholstery kits usually include auxiliary items as well as the covering. Hampton Coach's seat kits, for example, contain cotton padding and burlap to make them ready to install on your springs and frame. Headliner kits come with windlace, cording, and wire-on; panel kits are sewn and glued to new backing board; convertible interior kits include the top well pieces.

Firms marketing upholstery and supplies for later models carry new, molded seat foam along with their pre-sewn covers. Side wall panels come

Cotton batting is intended to be torn to shape and size, not cut. You can stuff it into holes in the coarse material covering seat springs to renew and even the surface.

ready to install, with fabric covering and holes for hardware marked to cut out. On some you have to swap the stainless trim from the old panel. Reproduction dash pads, pre-cut package shelf board, insulation kits, armrest pads, sun visors, and many other interior parts can make interior restoration of the more popular car models an easy, at-home undertaking. Write for catalogs. Then spend an evening making up a want list of ready-to-install equipment. With that done, you can make another list of the things that aren't available by mail order or over the counter.

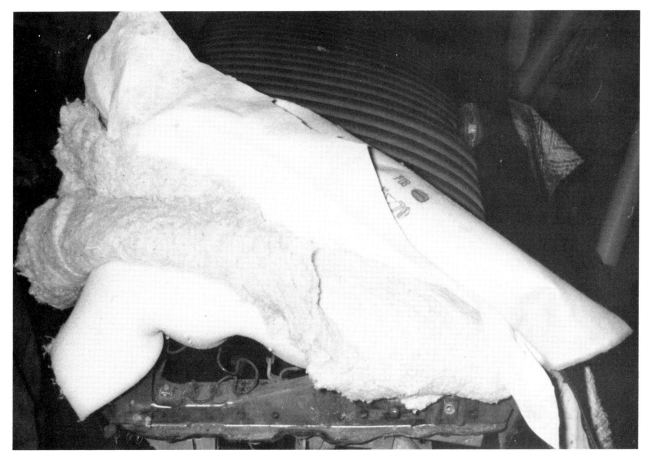

Some seat padding consists of a layer of soft foam covered with a layer of cotton batting. The cover material has a thin foam backing to provide a uniform surface.

Padding Materials

The question of "how original?" crops up even when considering unseen things like seat padding. Because their thirties or forties convertible seats were padded with cotton, many restorers insist that they be restored the same way. Others may prefer to work with foam rubber or a modern synthetic batting material.

Cotton

Until foam rubber came into widespread use in the sixties, cotton batting provided the cushioning and shape for auto seats. Side walls also often were padded with a thin layer of cotton.

Cotton batting comes in sheets usually an inch thick, twenty-seven inches wide, and rolled into a bundle. It is easily torn to fit the size and shape of the seat cushion or back. Pieces can be torn off and stuffed into seats to restore fullness and fill hollow spots. Consider that cotton mats down to about one-fourth its original thickness within a few months, so while it will continue to function as a foundation, it may not contribute as much to the fullness of the seat.

Dacron Polyester

This synthetic material has replaced some of the cotton (and formerly wool) batting in upholstery. It is an acceptable substitute if you don't want to buy both for your project. Dacron's most popular size is one inch thick and twenty-seven inches wide with thirty-nine to forty-five yards of material in a roll, but you can buy smaller quantities from an upholstery shop.

Dacron polyester is very soft and compressible. It retains more springiness than cotton but eventually mats down in the same way. It is a fine final-surface padding, providing a desired resilience as long as it is not compressed by pulling the cover too tightly. Wads of Dacron can also fill out spots where the cover is too loose.

While both are made of Dacron fiber, the batting or wrap is a totally different product from Dacron woven into soft, smooth-finish cover fabric.

Foam

The foam found in the upholstery industry, while referred to as foam rubber, is actually plastic by virtue of its manufacturing process. I refer to it simply as foam in this discussion.

Rolls in this vinyl seat cover are being padded with soft one-inch foam. Scrim, the light fabric material sewn to *the back side, prevents the stitching from pulling through the foam.*

You can use Dacron or polyester mat for padding in place of cotton batting. It can be applied in sheets, as shown, or torn or cut into pieces and stuffed in as needed.

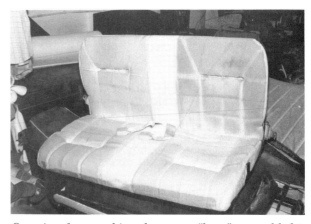

One-piece foam cushions known as "buns" are molded to shape for late-model car seats. Replacements are available if yours are worn out.

The two properties of foam you need to be concerned with are density and firmness. Density, measured in pounds per cubic foot (PCF), indicates the thickness of the cell walls which contain the air pockets that give foam its springiness. A higher PCF number means thicker cell walls and longer life. Your seating foam will be in the range of 1.40 to 2.0pcf.

A foam density rating of under 1.20pcf means a relatively short life, 1.40 to 1.60pcf moderate longevity, and 1.80 to 2.0-plus has the greatest longevity.

Foam comes in various thicknesses and densities and is easily cut with a hacksaw blade. Two or more sheets can be glued together to create greater thicknesses.

The measure of firmness, or load-bearing capacity, is known as "Indentation Load Deflection" (ILD) and gauges how much the foam compresses under a given weight. The higher the ILD rating, the firmer the foam, but interpretation varies with the use of the foam.

For seat backs, an ILD rating of twelve to fourteen is considered soft; sixteen to eighteen, medium; twenty to twenty-four, firm; and twenty-six and above, extra firm. On the seat cushion, twenty to twenty-four is soft; twenty-six to thirty, medium; thirty-two to thirty-six, firm; thirty-eight to forty-five, extra firm; and forty-six and above, super firm.

Firmness and density should be carefully considered when repadding seats. For most purposes, two different grades, one of medium to hard firmness for supportive padding and build-up and a softer one for finish padding, should be sufficient. Those with a higher density rating are preferable for seating, but not as necessary for padding door and side panels.

Foam comes in a variety of forms. As mentioned, preformed seat cushions known as "buns" are available for many common models from the sixties up. Foam sheets up to one inch thick are rolled, while thicker forms come in blocks two to five (or more) inches thick. Since foam is manufactured in huge blocks, it can be sliced to any size and thickness.

Dismantling the original interior and noting where foam is used, or where it might be substituted for the original material, will give you a good idea of your foam needs. Generally, you'll need a supply of soft, one-inch foam for surface padding. Rather than buying several sizes of firmer material, get a sufficient quantity of one-inch or two-inch blocks, which can be layered to create the desired thickness.

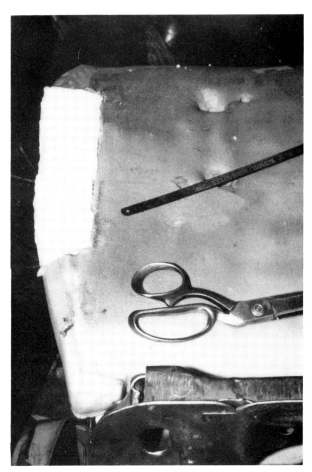

Trim out a damaged section of foam, cut new foam to shape and glue it into the hole. Trim the patch to the approximate shape, and it will not be noticeable with the cover in place.

Foam padding is also offered in a variety of special forms which may make your job easier. Some is pre-molded in channels of various widths to facilitate laying out and sewing up a roll-and-pleat design, for instance. When padding must be sewn, a backing is needed to hold the thread so it doesn't pull through. For such a purpose, foam in 1/4in and 1/2in thicknesses is available with a light muslin or paper backing attached.

You can also make cloth-backed foam at home by gluing a thin sheet of foam to a woven cloth such as muslin, or even an old bed sheet or window curtain. A 1/2in thickness next to the outside covering affords enough padding to give definition to a sewn-in design or pattern.

If you're working on a fairly recent model car, the molded foam seat padding may need only rejuvenation. It can be puffed up, and the shape and resilience restored, by applying steam with a steamer, tea kettle, or steam iron to areas that have stiffened. Be careful not to touch a hot iron or utensil to the foam, as it will melt.

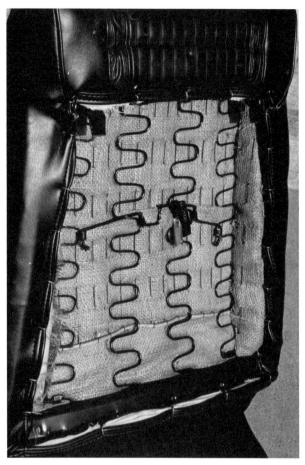

Coarse and strong, burlap keeps springs from damaging the padding. Pull it over and attach it to the seat frame with hog rings to form a base for the padding.

Ready-to-install welt cord comes in a variety of materials and colors. It has a sewing allowance of about 3/8in and cuts about every 1/4in to facilitate bending around corners.

Chunks of the molded cushion may be fragmented or torn out in high-wear areas like the outer edges of the driver's seat. Cut out these sections to leave even surfaces on all sides. Then cut a piece of foam of similar density to fit the hole and glue it into place.

Burlap

For years burlap filled the upholsterer's need for a tough, inexpensive material to cover seat springs and prevent their flexing from shifting or damaging the padding. This coarse, natural material is sold in rolls; old potato sacks that have been cleaned will also serve the purpose.

Seats that are in good condition may not need new burlap. If yours require rebuilding or spring replacement, pay attention to how the burlap is fitted and attached so you can put new material on the same way. Usually it is pulled snugly over the springs, wrapped over the outside rim of the seat frame and attached to it with hog rings.

Seat padding kits combining burlap and cotton padding are offered by some suppliers to simplify the seat re-covering process.

Panel Board

Door and side panel upholstery attaches to a fiberboard known as "panel board" or "upholstery board," which is held onto the door or body by spring clips (usually), tacks or screws, or a combination of these. Moisture accumulation over the years often rots away at least the bottom portion and may have warped the board.

Upholstery supply houses carry waterproof panel board, which is treated to resist the damaging effects of moisture. There are pre-cut panels available for particular models, but you may have to cut panels out of a larger sheet. Save what remains of the panels you take off as patterns for making new ones. If no panels exist, make patterns out of heavy, clear plastic. Tape the plastic to the door or area to be covered, draw the outline and hardware hole locations with a marker and cut out.

Some professional trimmers prefer 1/8in Masonite over panel board because it offers a more rigid foundation. To minimize possible moisture or humidity damage, seal whatever panel board you choose with two or three coats of a preservative

Panel board forms a semi-rigid base for door and side panel upholstery.

such as Thompson Water Seal or Weldwood Woodlife. A saber saw or jigsaw will be required to cut Masonite panels, but upholstery shears or tin snips will suffice for panel board.

Again, check with suppliers for your particular vehicle. Some carry reproduction panels, upholstered and ready to install, for certain models. On the other hand, some cars from the sixties and later may have panels molded from fiberboard or fiberglass which are not being reproduced. In that case, you may have to improvise a way of repairing the panel or find a better one in a salvage yard. I'll cover some tips later on.

Welting

A welt is a small roll or bead which adds strength to a seam or edge, or decorates or highlights a design in the fabric cover. Welt cord is made in sizes from 3/32in to 6/32in. Original-style welting consists of a core of white plastic, a tissue material or jute inside a cover material, usually vinyl, that matches or contrasts with the upholstery fabric. Contemporary welting comes in a number of colors as an extruded, flexible plastic with a hollow center. Although you can make welt cord, using a ready-made cord is much easier.

Windlace

Windlace, the roll that forms a seal around door openings, is covered with upholstery fabric to harmonize with the side wall upholstery. Again, several suppliers to the restoration trade stock authentic original windlace ready to install or as woven fabric to cover windlace core. One type that's apparently not being reproduced is the woven vinyl used in many 1965 Chryslers and some other sixties cars.

If you have to make your own windlace, upholstery trade suppliers have the rubber core material in rolls.

Adhesives

Many upholstery adhesives are available. You may want to check with a trim supply house about special formulations for specific applications, but a couple types should be sufficient for the work you'll be doing. A 3M Company representative recommended their 8031 Fast Tack Adhesive for cloth material and 8090 Super Trim Adhesive for vinyl. 3M's 8046 Top & Trim Adhesive, which comes only in bulk, can be used where a stronger bond is required. Their 8080 General Trim Adhesive is a good, all-around product for a variety of materials

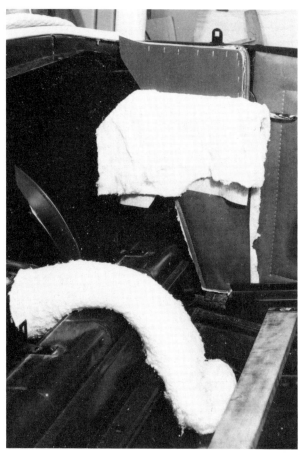

To be authentic, cotton batting should be installed on early cars. LeBaron Bonney supplies it with their re-upholstery kits like this one for a 1931 Model A roadster.

Cotton padding covered with vinyl or leather results in a smooth, cushioned shoulder panel.

found in the car's interior. Similar products are available from other manufacturers like Rhinyl Products and Camie/Kingco.

Some things to be aware of: a product like Fast Tack sets up quickly, but stays tacky for some time so it can be pulled loose and repositioned. Super Trim Adhesive is a contact cement, applied to both surfaces, and may take an hour to set up to the optimum bonding point. Top & Trim Adhesive, Super Trim Adhesive and, to a lesser extent, General Trim Adhesive are compounded to counteract the properties of vinyl plastics that can soften and weaken some adhesives. Convenience is also a factor. Some types of adhesive come in aerosol containers, while others are sold only in bulk for brushing on or using a spray gun.

The recommended type of adhesive is specified in some places in this book, not in others. Use common sense regarding the location of the installation and the amount of stress the adhesive must endure. Where a strong bond is required—a piece under stress and hanging by the glue—use a stronger product and apply it as contact cement. That is, put it on both surfaces and allow it to set

up before pressing the two pieces together. If there is little stress on a panel, such as a door panel where staples or clips help hold the covering in place, a single coat of a general trim adhesive should be sufficient. Read and follow the directions on the container.

For small tasks and repairs, aerosol spray cans are handy and easy to use. Adhesives can also be purchased in bulk and applied with a paint brush. If you're undertaking a complete interior job and have an air compressor, a spray gun system is an efficient way of applying a bulk adhesive.

Tools

Basic mechanic and household tools such as pliers, wrenches, screwdrivers, a tack hammer, electric drill and saber saw, will be needed to accomplish your upholstery job. A good pair of upholstery shears is a must for the amount of cutting required; household scissors just aren't adequate.

Although a wooden yardstick will suffice, a steel straightedge up to five feet long will make marking easier; a large square is valuable, too.

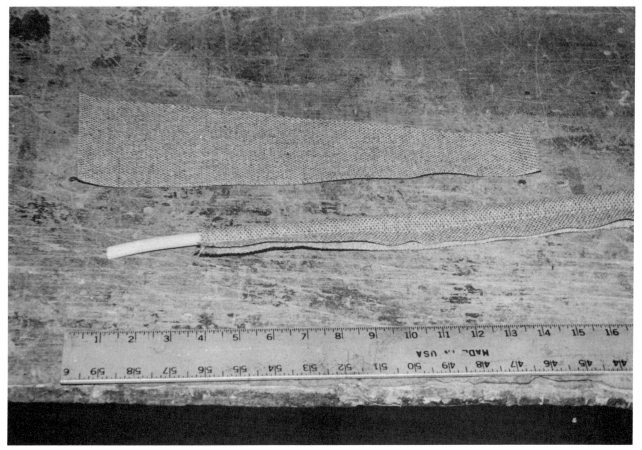

Ready-made windlacing is available for many interior restorations. You can also make your own by gluing fabric around a rubber core. Sewing is also recommended if a welt foot is available to get the seam tight against the rubber core.

Chalk shaped into a sharp wedge is fine for marking dark material; a soft lead pencil is useful for lighter shades. Tailor's chalk is also available. Don't use a ball-point pen on a cover material as the ink will bleed through.

A utility knife or hobby knife will be needed to cut foam and for other trimming. An electric carving knife (don't let your spouse catch you!) works great for cutting and shaping blocks of foam, but a hacksaw blade is also good. Hog-ring pliers are necessary for attaching the rings that hold seat covers on. A 1/4in punch is useful to cut holes in panel board for trim and hardware. An awl or ice pick is handy to locate holes through fabric and to punch holes for buttons and trim. If you don't have a staple gun, plan to rent one for the panel work.

Hardware and Fasteners

When dismantling your car's interior in preparation for its new trim job, be sure to keep all the clips, trim screws, tacks, and other fasteners you remove. Put them in separate containers and identify them. Egg cartons are handy to keep different fasteners separate. Even if they're not reusable, you will know exactly what to get as replacements. Some common fasteners will be obtainable at your local hardware store, but many specialized items are available only from upholstery specialty suppliers. Firms serving the restoration trade usually carry the necessary correct fasteners and hardware. If you order a kit for all or part of your interior, it should include the right fasteners.

Get a supply of staples for your staple gun to attach covering to panel boards. For strength, use the longest staples that don't go entirely through the panel board. Upholstery may also be stapled to a wood framework or to tack strips in earlier models.

A supply of 3/4in hog rings will be needed for attaching seat covering. Some long upholsterer's pins are handy for securing material in place before sewing.

Seat Springs

Newer seats, except those made with molded foam padding, have zigzag springs, known as "sinuous" or "no-sag," for cushion support. Earlier cars had coil springs joined together into cushion units. Both types of springs are available from uphol-

Besides the usual mechanic and household tools, a few specialized tools like this pneumatic staple gun make upholstery work easier.

stery supply houses, if needed to replace ones that are broken or sagging from years of wear.

Some antique auto supply houses carry complete reproduction spring units as well as complete seats.

If buttons are part of your interior design, check to see if ready-made buttons are available, or if a supplier will make them to order in your chosen fabric. Otherwise, consider a button making machine. They start at under $100. Button molds come in popular sizes from 9/16in to one inch diameter.

Nylon thread is recommended for your sewing jobs, although Dacron or polyester are also good. They're strong and non-organic to resist decay. Have a spool of hand sewing thread and at least one good curved needle on hand for repairing or finishing. Thread comes in any color to blend with your covering material. You may also need nylon tufting twine for tying in buttons.

Insulation

One thing your older car probably doesn't have much of is insulation. Consider adding it during the interior rebuild. Great advances have been made in insulating materials during the last 20 years, partly because of the space program. You can take advantage of these products to shield your car's interior from heat, cold, and noise. It hides behind the upholstery, so picky show judges won't even have to know it's there.

Insulating the firewall, floor, and transmission tunnel can cut out a lot of heat from the engine compartment and exhaust system. Jute carpet padding, used in the automotive industry for years, is still one of the best and cheapest materials to shield heat and sound.

A product called Cerablanket, developed by Johns-Manville to insulate furnaces, does a good job on the firewall and transmission tunnel, but it can crush underfoot if used on the floor. Glue it to the back of carpet or other material before attaching the material to the body.

Kool Kar, Rodsulation and Cool-It are some of the trade names for a family of space-age insulation products. Generally, they consist of air pockets sealed between layers of aluminized materials. They may come in rolls or sheets that can be cut to size and installed with trim adhesive to the inside surfaces of door, side and roof panels. These mod-

Replacements for sagging zigzag (shown) and coil springs are available.

ern materials are better than the cotton and composition material originally used in cars, and they don't absorb moisture, which can lead to rust.

Rubberized undercoating available in aerosol cans from auto or paint supply outlets will help insulate against heat and sound. Apply it to the under side of the floorboards and inside door and side panels. Tight-fitting grommets around wires, hoses and linkage passing through the firewall will help seal out heat from the engine compartment. Use metal push plugs (available at electronics stores), duct tape, or caulk to fill holes and gaps in the firewall.

Sewing Machine

This item is more likely than any other to stop automotive hobbyists from tackling their own upholstery jobs! Upholstery means sewing, something they know nothing about and have little interest in learning. When an upholstery sewing machine comes to mind, the image is of a large, expensive commercial machine.

That's not necessarily the case. Many popular cloth fabrics are light enough to sew on a good quality home machine adapted for the job with a heavy duty needle and presser foot. Leather and vinyl will require a heavier duty machine, however. One of the suppliers listed in the Appendix offers a reasonably priced compact machine that will handle most upholstery tasks.

What you're looking for, besides the capacity to sew several layers of heavy material or sew through panel board, is a walking foot, which helps pull the material through the machine. A welting foot, which permits stitching right up next to welt cord or windlace core, is a useful option if you plan to make your own welt or windlace. Reversible action isn't a necessity, but it can be convenient for intricate stitching and to use at the end of a seam to set the thread and keep it from pulling out.

Much of an upholstery job can be done without sewing, especially with the ready-made seat covers, headliners, side wall panels, and other upholstered pieces available for many popular makes and models. Covering is usually glued and/or stapled to door, side panel, and other panels. Carpet edging, if needed, can be done by hand.

Some sewing machine dealers and equipment rental firms have commercial machines you can

53

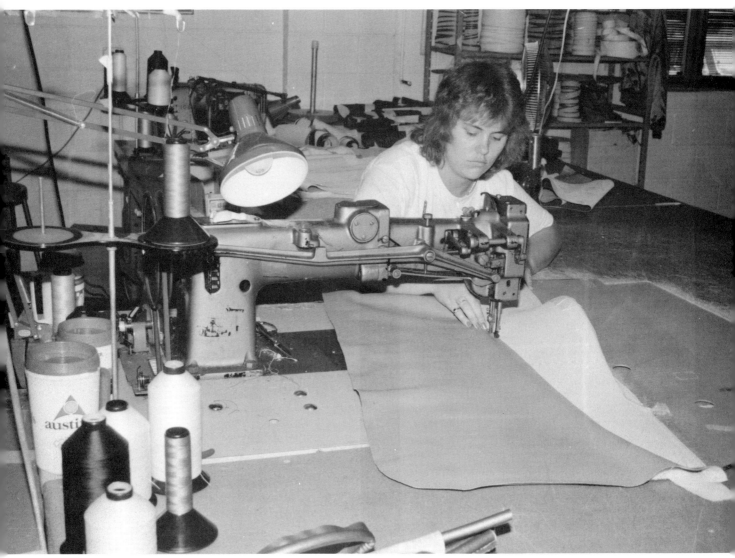

You might rent a sewing machine or farm out that part of the work, but you can do much upholstery work without a machine. A spacious area is needed to lay out your work.

rent for the necessary sewing. Be sure everything is ready to go so you don't have to keep it any longer than necessary. An alternative is to lay out your seat covering, headliner or whatever and take it to a commercial shop to be sewn up.

Whatever the choice, don't let the lack of an industrial sewing machine deter you from doing your own upholstery work.

Work Area

A fairly large and clean work area is a must for any upholstery job. You need room to lay out large sheets of material for measuring, marking and cutting. Close proximity to the car isn't necessary, but it is helpful when measuring and fitting pieces individually. A 4x8ft panel of 1/2in plywood set over a pair of sawhorses in the garage provides an adequate work area, but be sure to clean or cover the floor to prevent soiling your material. Consider a cheap, old carpet from a thrift store. A board laid over a pool or Ping-Pong table can also serve as a work site.

Make a checklist of the materials and supplies you'll require and have everything on hand when you begin. That way you won't be delayed while waiting for a needed component or tool.

Chapter Six

Upholstery Techniques

Upholstering, like most crafts, is a matter of learning a few basic procedures, then applying them in various combinations to create a finished product. Once learned, the basic techniques of working with upholstery fabric can be applied to making seat covers, side wall panels, headliners, and all the other passenger compartment and trunk furnishings.

Materials and ways of using them in the upholstery trade change and improve constantly. While automakers of the thirties and forties were limited to cotton batting for padding seats, foam or Dacron batting now do the job better. Most restorers want their cars to be as authentic as possible, but few object to upgrading as long as they can retain the original appearance.

In this book, I show mostly modern methods and materials. In some cases I will discuss the differences between these and the original procedures. The assumption here is that as long as the resulting upholstered piece looks and feels right, how it got that way is not important. A show judge isn't going to make you pull loose a seat cover to check what kind of filler you used.

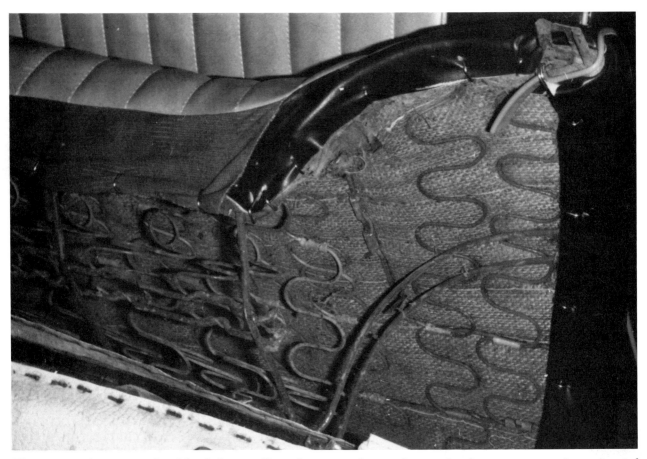

The exercise of removing the old upholstery will teach you much of what you need to know to put it back to-gether, such as noting how a seat cover is constructed and attached to the seat frame.

Naturally, you're free to use whatever materials you prefer. For the most part, the steps will be the same. So, if I talk about cutting and fitting a sheet of cloth-backed foam padding, you can substitute cotton batting and achieve the same result.

Also, there are often several ways of doing a particular job. The techniques shown in this book aren't the last word, but they are ones that work for the professional trimmers who are using them. Another trimmer may vary them or have an entirely different approach. In the process of disassembling your old interior, you may well discover a better or easier way to accomplish the task.

With all upholstering tasks, step one is to make a pattern, step two is to prepare the covering, and step three is to fit and attach it to the panel or seat. Since pleating, tufting, and other design techniques discussed in this chapter have to do with making the covering, we'll deal only with that aspect here. Except for instances in which the cover is constructed directly on the panel, applying the covering to the various interior components will be taken up in subsequent chapters.

Preparation

If you are totally refinishing the interior, start by removing all the old upholstery. This step is discussed in more detail in the chapters covering specific interior components, so it would be a good idea to look ahead to those sections before tearing into the tasks. If you're not doing a total job, remove only those parts being refinished plus any that restrict access to them.

The interior work must be done in a logical sequence so you don't find yourself having to tear out something because you forgot to put something else in first. If it will help, keep a notebook and write down the steps in it. Allow yourself as much working space as possible.

Determine exactly what parts are to be finished with what materials. Then make a pattern for each individual part and, from the patterns collectively, figure out how much material they will require.

Remove the seats for access to the interior, but wait to dismantle them until you are ready to work on them. Remove trim and garnish moldings and note how the headliner, side walls, and other panels are attached. As you remove them, save

Use the old pieces as patterns to lay out the new. It's especially critical when working with expensive material like this leather hide.

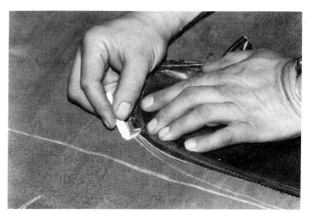

Mark places where cuts need to be made or seams intersect for reference when sewing the new panels.

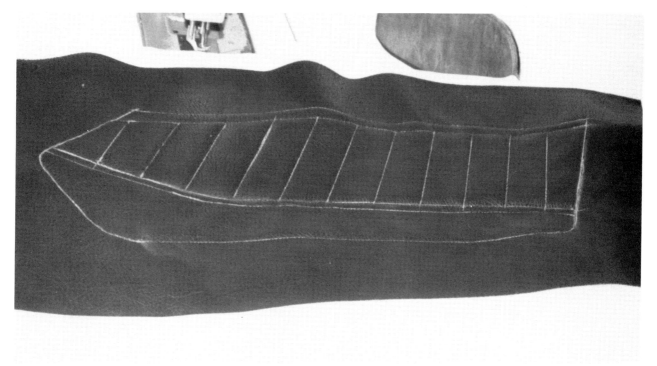

Draw the pattern to be stitched onto the outside of the cover material with chalk for dark materials, soft pencil for lighter material.

and identify all clips and fasteners. Leave the carpet until last; it will provide a soft work surface to work on and catch any screws you drop.

Make a Pattern

Like a good tailor, you should begin your interior layout by making patterns of each part and panel to be upholstered. For a start, separate all the individual pieces at the seams and identify each one with a code, such as FSC for front seat cushion and FSB for front seat back. Number the

headliner panels from front to rear. If some pieces are to be finished in one type of fabric and others in another, separate and stack them accordingly. These pieces may serve as patterns provided they are not stretched, shrunk, or badly misshapen.

Paper patterns may work better and are easy to make. Roll out a length of heavy paper and trace the outline of each piece onto it with an indelible marker. Where possible, trace around the rigid panel rather than the fabric cover, but remember to draw a second line for cutting about

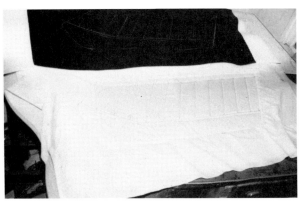

Sew foam and backing cloth together in the same pattern as the cover. The backing here is a paper cloth often used by upholsterers, but muslin, an old bed sheet, or any cloth that will hold the stitches will work.

two inches outside the first line to provide the edge that folds over and attaches to the panel. Allow an extra inch for seams on pieces of fabric that are to be sewn together.

When working with two kinds or colors of fabric, make the patterns for one on brown wrapping paper and for the other on white butcher paper. Identify each part and, if it's a factor, note the direction the cover has to lie.

If there's no old piece to serve as a pattern, cover that section with a heavy piece of clear plastic and trace the outline onto it with a marker, including any openings and attachment points. Mark the locations of hardware such as door handles, window cranks, and decorative trim on your patterns. To aid in placement of the cover or a design, such as a pleated section or an insert, draw in the side-to-side and top-to-bottom center lines of each panel.

Using the original covering, sketch the panel's design onto the pattern. If the upholstery was missing or incorrect, you may have to rely upon photographs, sales literature, or someone else's measurements to reproduce the correct design. Use a pencil at first so you can erase and make changes until the layout is right. Then trace over it with a marker.

If a panel has rolls and pleats or button tufting, draw that design onto the pattern, measuring carefully to be sure it is correctly located. More detail on this procedure will follow. Determine where sections of different material or colors go, and show them on the patterns with markers of corresponding colors.

When you work out a particular measurement, such as the width of rolls or depth of a certain panel, write it on the pattern for quick reference later. Make notes in the margin to remind you of other points to consider when making up the upholstery cover. Having a pattern for every piece will ensure that nothing is overlooked.

Estimate Material Requirements

Your patterns will be your best tool for accurately determining the amounts of material (padding as well as cover fabric) your job will take. Place all the pieces to come out of one type of fabric onto another large sheet of paper, and arrange them to make the best use of the material with a minimum of waste. Make your layout the width of the fabric, which is usually fifty-four inches. When all the parts are accounted for on this model, measuring the length covered gives you the number of yards of fabric required.

Get one or two yards extra to provide a margin for error in cutting; allow more for pleats and tufts. For example, a seat cushion fifty-four inches wide may require seventy-two inches of material for deep tufts or pleats. As a rough estimate, front and rear seats together require ten to twelve yards of material, a headliner four or five yards, and an entire sedan interior twenty to twenty-five yards.

Something else to bear in mind before cutting or sewing is any directional consideration of your fabric. If it has a nap, like velour, run your hand over it to see what direction the nap lies. Stroked one way it is smooth and velvety, the opposite way coarse and bristly. It's like stroking a cat; the fur lies down smooth when you pet it head to toe, but stroked backwards, the fur goes in all directions—and irritates the cat!

For the color and sheen to look correct and uniform, a napped fabric must be applied so that the nap falls down like the flow of a waterfall. It feels smooth when stroked from top to bottom on side panels and seat backs and from back to front on seat cushions. It stays cleaner, to, because it tends to shed, rather than trap, dust and soil.

The pattern of upholstery covering must also be considered. The ribs of a Bedford Cord must run in the correct direction. Broadcloth may have stripes or brocade a pattern that must run in a certain direction to correctly duplicate the original interior.

Vinyl may get its direction from a particular grain pattern, so be sure the pattern is applied in the same direction on all panels. Most vinyl stretches more in one direction than another, so this is a factor in how it's applied. Like vinyl, leather may have an embossed pattern that will determine the direction it should be installed.

Unless you have some experience working with fabrics and performing the procedures that follow, it would be wise to practice with scrap material such as an old sheet before attempting it with upholstery cloth. It also helps to make a small paper "model" of the piece to follow—anything to avoid a mistake that could ruin a piece of expensive fabric.

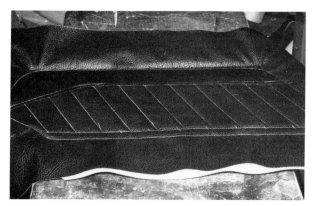

A cover topstitched to 1/2in foam and cloth backing has only a slight raised-roll effect, but sufficient to give definition to the panel design.

Tuck-and-Roll

"Tuck-and-roll" or "roll-and-pleat" are popular terms applied to an upholstery design that's been common throughout the years. "Channeling" is another term for this design, although it is applied more in the furniture trimming trade.

A pleat is a fold made when the material is turned back upon itself and secured in that position. On a seat cover the pleat in the outer covering is sewn to a flexible backing material. On a side wall panel it may be either sewn or stapled to the panel board.

In earlier times, the cover fabric was left loose between pleats, then stuffed with cotton, foam, or Dacron padding, and this approach is still preferred for an authentic look. A more modern method is to secure the pleat through a sheet of foam to the backing. The foam provides the puff of the roll, or channel. The pleat is tucked down between the rolls.

Pressed Pleats

When vinyl came into widespread use in production cars, so did pressed pleats. The roll-and-pleat pattern is pressed into the vinyl cover by a heat process. Original pressed pleat patterns are available for many popular models in reproduction seat covers and side panels. Even if these ready-made items aren't available to fit your car, you may be able to locate pre-pleated material to make them.

If you have to start from scratch, there's still help that trimmers in an earlier day didn't have: foam padding with the rolls and pleats pressed in. Just sew along the channels. There's less measuring, no need to draw out the design, and no stuffing of individual rolls.

Auto interior designers have used rolls of many widths, from an inch or less to several inches. The most common are between one and three inches. Although ordinarily thought of as even and parallel, they can also be done in irregular straight lines, varying widths or curves. Fullness varies according to the thickness of the padding and how each roll is finished. Some are mainly for visual effect while others help provide a seat's cushioning quality. We'll look at several ways of making rolls, from simple to complex, thin to fat.

Topstitching

You'll want to duplicate the manufacturer's methods as closely as possible. If, for example, the original car had vinyl pressed pleats and the necessary material is unavailable, you can come close by topstitching the pleats.

On the back of the cover material mark the outline of the panel. Then measure where pleats are to be sewn. This measurement will be the width of the roll plus 1/2in for the sewn or stapled pleat plus any allowance for fullness of the roll. Draw lines where the pleats are to be sewn or stapled. The material will be folded on these lines to form the pleats.

Cut out the cover material, allowing one to two inches top and bottom and the width of an extra roll or two on each end for attachment to the panel or other components.

Mark pleat lines on the foam backing the exact width of the desired rolls.

Topstitching is widely practiced in the new car industry, and it's quite simple to do. However, it's not always the most durable. For one thing, puncturing the cover material by sewing weakens it along the stitch line, and flexing over a period of time can cause it to split. Also, the stitches hold only one layer, and the thread is exposed to wear. Often the thread wears out and lets go while the cover fabric or vinyl remains in good shape.

Pre-channeled foam is the easiest to work with if you can get the correct channel width. Then it's simply a matter of marking the face of the cover material with stitch lines to match the channels in the foam and sewing along them.

If you're starting from scratch, cut your cover material—a sheet of 1/4in or 1/2in foam and backing material—slightly larger than the pattern for the piece you're making. Backing material can be any tightly woven fabric that will hold the stitches; cloth-backed foam is available to make the job easier. Glue cover, foam, and backing together to keep them from shifting.

Draw the tuck-and-roll design from your pattern onto the face of the cover material, extending the lines all the way to the edge of the piece. Sew along the middle line first. Move to the next line and so on to one edge. Then return to the center and work out to the other edge. Finally, sew around the outer perimeter of the rolled panel. When it is ready to be joined to another panel, you can trim the edge as necessary to make it easier to work with.

If the original upholstery had sharper definition or thicker rolls, use correspondingly thicker foam padding, and add to the cover material measurement to account for the fullness of the rolls. To tuck the cover material down into the foam and make stitching easier, slit the foam with a razor half or three-fourths of the way through (don't cut all the way), and press the cover into the crack before sewing. Hold the slit open with your fingers as you direct the material through the machine, being careful to follow the stitch line marked on the cover.

Some upholsterers follow the above approach, slitting the foam to about 1/2in from the backing, to topstitch deeper tucks and fuller rolls with padding one or two inches thick. Starting in the middle, the cover is folded along the marked stitch line and the fold inserted into the slit, tucked down as far as it will go and held with two or three upholsterer's pins. When all tucks are done the same way, they are topstitched by spreading the slit open enough for the material to go through the machine. If your machine will handle it, this is a good method, because the padding closes over the seam, both hiding and protecting the thread from wear.

Layout and Measurement

The above method and those to follow require some different measuring, so we'll cover that here before going on to sewn and stapled pleats.

If the padding is to be more than 1/2in thick, you need to allow for the fullness of the rolls. Cut a strip of padding the width of the roll, 1-1/2in, for example, or mark two lines that distance apart on a block of foam or sheet of Dacron filling. Lay the cover material over it, and have a helper pull the material down tight into the foam exactly on the

two marks or around the strip of padding, simulating the arc of the finished roll. Follow the arc with a piece of paper, marking it at the bottom of each depression. Lay the paper flat and measure between the two marks to find out how much material to allow for the fullness of each roll.

When pleats are to be sewn or stapled, allow an additional 1/2in, the amount needed to fold over and form each pleat. In this example the roll width, 1-1/2in, plus 1/2in for the pleat and, say, another 1/2in for fullness, makes 2-1/2in of material required for each roll.

To follow this example through, let's say the panel to be covered is thirty-two inches wide. Thirty-two divided by 1-1/2in (the width of each finished roll) equals twenty-one, the number of rolls to cover the panel plus a fraction left over at each end. Transfer these measurements to the padding. Mark the outside lines thirty-two inches apart (leaving some extra on each end) and the center line, which will be sixteen inches from each end.

If there were to be an even number of rolls in the panel, there would be an equal number on each

Fold the cover along the pleat line, align the fold with the line on the foam backing, and sew 1/8 to 1/4in from

the fold. Begin at the end of the panel that will be most visible and work across to the other end.

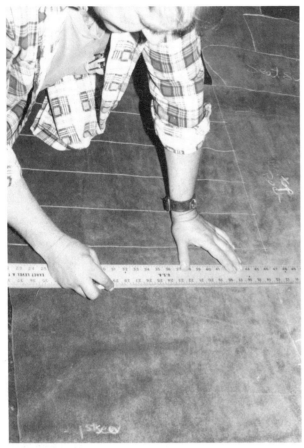

The finished rolls for this Hudson seat cover are to be three inches wide. Norm Kyhn marked the pleat lines on the back of the leather 3-3/4in apart to allow 3/4in for sewing and fullness.

The exact three-inch roll width is drawn onto the muslin backing.

After cutting out the leather panel, Norm folded it on the first pleat line, aligned the fold with the first pleat line on the muslin backing, and sewed 1/4in from the folded edge.

Rolls on the finished panel are loose and will be stuffed with filling individually. Notice how the pleats fold the same direction. This must be consistent throughout the car.

side of the center line. Taking the example of twenty-one rolls, an odd number, the center line falls in the middle of the center roll. The roll, 1-1/2 inches wide, divided by two equals 3/4 inch, the distance on

either side of the center line where the first pleats must go. Measure and draw these lines onto the foam. Then measure out in 1-1/2-inch increments in each direction, drawing a parallel line at each point.

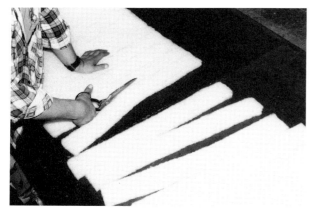

Measure out and mark filling material for the width of the rolls, three inches in the case of the Hudson seat cover. Cut the filler strips. In this case bonded Dacron is being used in place of the original cotton.

Pockets in the muslin backing could have been left open, but Norm Kyhn feels he gets a better look by sewing the top and bottom edges, then cutting the pockets open just inside the stitch lines, top and bottom.

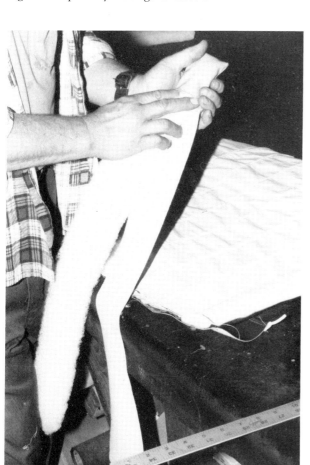

Insert a filler strip into a "sock" made of a strip of vinyl folded over and sewn on one end.

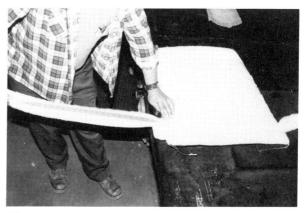

Shove the sock and filler through the pocket with a smooth stick like the yardstick shown. It will slip through easily if you turn the smooth side of the vinyl sock toward the leather.

The folds of the pleats fall on these lines.

The same thing must be done with the cover material, but on it the pleat lines must be 2-1/2in apart to take into account the allowances for full-

ness and pleating. On the back side of the fabric, mark the side-to-side center line of the piece, then measure out 1-1/4in on either side for the first pleats and in 2-1/2in increments in both directions for the remaining pleats. Also draw in the top and bottom line of the pleated panel on both fabric and foam, allowing two inches of border on each side.

Sewn Pleats

For sewn pleats, lay the cover material face down on a clean work table and mark the pleat lines onto the back side of the fabric with a soft lead pencil for light material or chalk for dark. Draw lines to indicate the top and bottom edges of the tuck-and-roll panel, then mark additional lines two inches outside the first for the sewing or attachment allowance. Measure and mark the exact center of the material, side to side. Measure and draw out your pleat pattern from the center reference point.

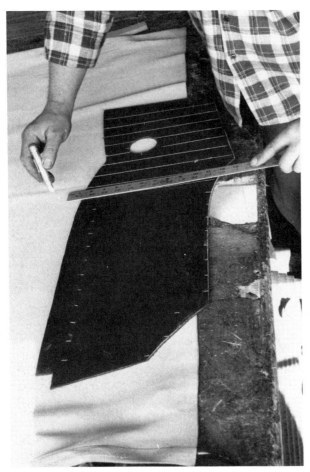

A tuck-and-roll cover can be constructed directly on a piece of panel board. Measure and mark the pleat lines on the board at the desired finished roll width. Cut the board to the exact size and shape.

Measure and mark the pleats on the back side of the cover material. Beginning at the end of the panel that will be most visible, fold the first pleat and line it up with the first pleat line on the board. Place a 1/4-inch strip of light cardboard along the fold to form a straight, even line and provide another surface for the staples to grip. Staple along the middle of the strip at 1/2-inch intervals.

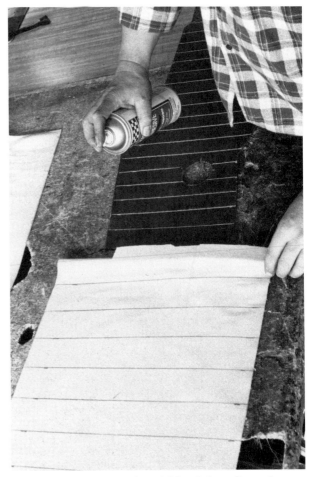

Cut foam into strips the width of the rolls and spray with upholstery adhesive. Also apply adhesive to the panel board.

Most tuck-and-roll jobs on seats were quite heavily padded. We'll get to those in a minute. For lightly padded side panels the pleats can be sewn directly onto a sheet of cloth-backed padding the desired thickness and glued to the panel board or, if you are using a commercial machine, both cover and padding can be sewn directly onto the panel board. On some seats where the roll-and-pleat pattern is mostly decorative, the pleats are sewn into the cover and through the cloth-backed padding, then installed on the seats over a thicker layer of padding.

Fold the cover material over on the first pleat line, line it up with the first stitchline marked on the padding and sew along 1/8in from the fold. Continue across the piece, sewing each pleat in the same manner. When all pleats have been sewn, sew across the top and bottom lines to secure the edges and help hold the pleats in shape.

When making up several pleated pieces for an interior, remember to face all the pleats in the same direction for a neat, professional appearance. For example, if pleats on the seat cushions face to

When adhesive becomes tacky, glue the foam strip to the board, just covering the previously stapled pleat.

This custom job has a welt of a contrasting color sewn into each pleat before attachment to the panel board.

the left, they should also face to the left on the backs. All the side panel pleats should face either to the front or the rear.

Hand Stuffing Rolls

When the rolls are to be padded an inch thick or more, you can control the width and shape and sew straighter lines if you sew the cover first, then go back and stuff the individual rolls. The old-time upholsterers did it this way—painstakingly, with cotton.

Following this procedure is necessary for true authenticity on some early models. One method is to use a piece of tubing—PVC plastic plumbing tubing, cardboard mailing tube, or even metal exhaust tubing—either whole or split in half. Fill the tube with cotton, insert it into the roll, then push the cotton out as you slowly withdraw the tube.

Another approach is to stuff individual wads of cotton into the sleeve with a probe.

A probe can be a flat strip of wood such as a yardstick or a wooden dowel. Round off the end and smooth all surfaces with sandpaper so it doesn't snag the material. The probe is also used to rearrange the filling for a smooth, lump-free roll.

Dacron batting is easier to use than cotton, holds its shape better, and hardly anyone can tell the difference. Strips of foam were used to pad some original tuck-and-roll jobs, so you may want to redo it the same way.

Cut the padding into strips the width of the rolls that have been sewn into the cover material with a muslin or other fabric backing. Slit the muslin just inside the perimeter stitching to open the top and bottom of each sleeve. Shove a strip

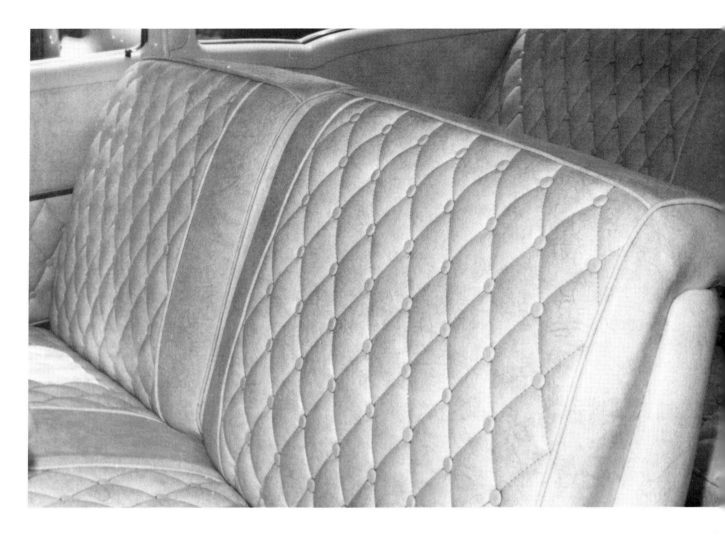

Above, a button tufted design must be laid out carefully. There may be a pre-quilted material available to match your original.

of padding through the sleeve. Making a vinyl pocket like the one pictured and using a straight-edge or yardstick to push it through the sleeve makes this job easier. Trim the ends of the padding strips.

Sewing the individual pleats over strips of padding one at a time is an alternative method for padding rolls. Follow the procedure outlined in the next section for stapled pleats, but sew instead of stapling.

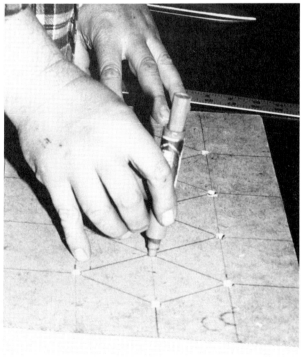

Left, to make a diamond-tufted panel, cut the panel board to size and draw the pattern onto the board. The center line should also be drawn (the vertical one is not drawn in this photo). Punch a 3/8in hole at each point where lines intersect and transfer the design to the chosen foam padding by tracing through the holes with a marker. Padding thickness will be determined by how puffy the tufts need to be.

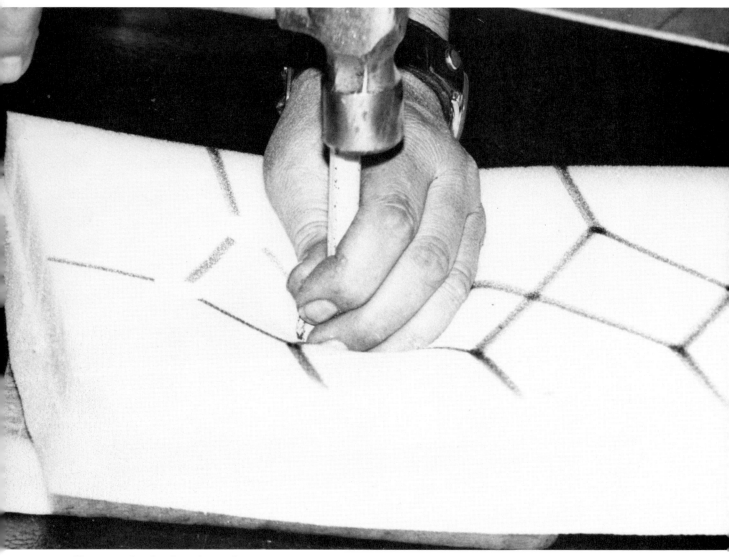

"Connect the dots" to draw the tuft pattern onto the foam. Punch holes in the foam slightly larger than the buttons to be used. For example, if the finished button *has a 5/8in diameter, make the holes 3/4in. A sharpened piece of tubing can be used as a punch.*

Stapled Pleats

Rolls and pleats can be done on side panels by stapling directly to the panel board instead of sewing. Sheet, cloth-backed, or pre-channeled foam will work equally well for padding. Lines designating the pleat locations must be drawn onto the panel board as well as the foam. Follow the procedure outlined above for sewn pleats, but instead of sewing, staple through the cover and foam onto the panel board.

An especially useful method for padding with thicker or firmer foam is to cut the foam into strips the exact width of each roll and slightly longer. Fold the cover material to form the first pleat at the end of the panel that will be most visible. Line up the fold with the corresponding line drawn on the panel board. Place a cardboard strip along the fold and staple down the middle of it.

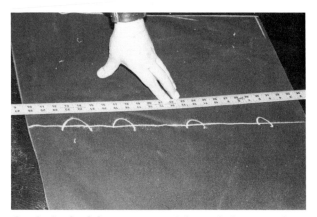

On the back of the cover material, mark the center lines in both directions. Allow plenty of material on all sides.

Begin inserting buttons at what will be the bottom center of the panel and work up and out to both sides. Push the button through the cover material (vinyl or leather must be punched first) and into the hole until it contacts the board and the prongs pass through the hole. Spread the prongs on the back side.

Apply trim adhesive to one foam strip and to the panel board where the first roll goes. Glue the foam strip into place with one edge just covering the stapled cardboard strip and the other lined up with the next mark on the panel board. Roll the material over the foam and fold along the next mark. Line this fold up with the next mark on the panel board, and staple down in the same manner as the first. Continue gluing a strip of foam and attaching a pleat at each line across the board.

Finish each end by gluing a strip of foam onto the last section, then pulling the covering snugly over it and around the edge of the panel board. Staple the cover on the back about 1/4in from the edge of the board. If the tuck-and-roll design extends to the edges of the panel, pull the cover over the top and bottom edges, being sure to pull any wrinkles out of the rolls, and staple in the same way. When finished, trim the excess material 1/2in from the staple line.

Tuck-and-Roll Variations

You could possibly have occasion to make a tuck-and-roll panel with two different colors or types of material. In this case, cut the material into strips the width of the roll plus an allowance for fullness and 1/2 to 3/4in for sewing. Place one strip face up and the next strip face down on top of it, lining up one edge. Sew the two strips together 1/4in from the edge. Fold the strip on top over so it is face up and attach the next strip in the same manner, and so on across the panel.

When the panel is sewn together, sew it to the backing material or staple to the panel board as described for sewn or stapled pleats, placing the stitch or staple line 1/8 to 1/4in inside the first stitches.

If a welt or piping is called for between pleats, cut strips of welt slightly longer than the pleats. Follow instructions outlined earlier for sewing pleats, but insert welt into each pleat. Sew or staple as close as possible to the welt cord.

Tufting

Tufted upholstery has appeared in cars in some form almost continuously. The words "button" and "tuft" are usually associated because but-

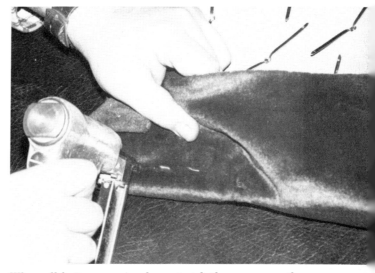

When all buttons are in place, stretch the cover over the edge of the board and staple on the back side.

Smooth folds between buttons with a probe made from a smooth wooden dowel.

Opposite page, Norm points to the starting point for button tufting this seat cushion. Begin at the back center and work forward and out.

ton tufted leather was common in early cars, as it had been in carriages. Those tuft designs are very deep and pronounced, while others are only moderately so. Tufting can also be accomplished without buttons, just as buttons can be incorporated in an upholstery scheme without actually creating tufts. We'll talk more about buttons a little later.

Diamond, half-diamond, square, and rectangular tufting patterns can all be constructed. Usually the button is inserted where the lines of the pattern intersect. The buttons or other decorations, or sometimes a piece of twine inserted through the material, pull the cover down into the padding to give the tufts their fullness.

Layout and Measurement

Careful design and layout are critical for a button tufted design to turn out well. The original cover, or even part of it, will be very useful to determine the correct original design. Lacking that, you may have to rely upon photos, sales literature, or measurements and diagrams from a similar model.

The design of an entire panel should be drawn out full size on heavy paper or directly on the backing material to be used—cloth for seat inserts, panel board for side walls. Locate the center, top to bottom, and side to side, and draw these lines in pencil or chalk for reference.

Draw the button and tuft pattern with locations of all buttons and the lines between. You can probably determine from the original how much definition the tufted surface should have, taking into

1960 Pontiac Ventura had a seat cover design incorporating rolls and pleats of varying widths in three different *colors plus welts and embossed emblems. The emblems were removed from the old covers and stitched to the new.*

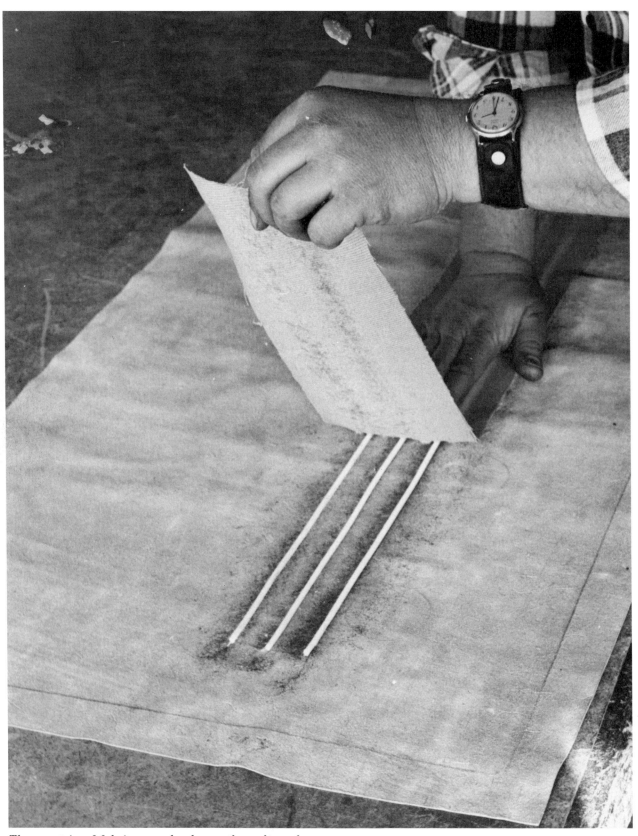

Then a strip of fabric was glued over the welt cord strips. This should be a tightly woven fabric that will hold stitches securely.

On a restoration project, Norm Kyhn had to reproduce three raised ribs on a leather door panel. He started by drawing the design on the back of the leather laid out to cover the panel.

account the matting down and loss of fullness from years of use. Without a good sample of the original, you may have to estimate. Padding on seats, for example, is heavier than on side walls.

Surface Design

We'll try to take the process of creating a button and tuft design in sequence from the simple to the complex. You can determine which fits your situation by the way the original was done.

The simplest solution, of course, would be to find cover material with the correct color, finish, and pattern already applied. Suppliers to the re-trimming trade do offer both vinyls and velours and possibly some other materials with diamond, square, or rectangular patterns pressed in. This kind of material has only a surface design with no more than 1/4 or 1/2in of padding. Buttons can be added if appropriate.

Some upholstery has a surface design creat-

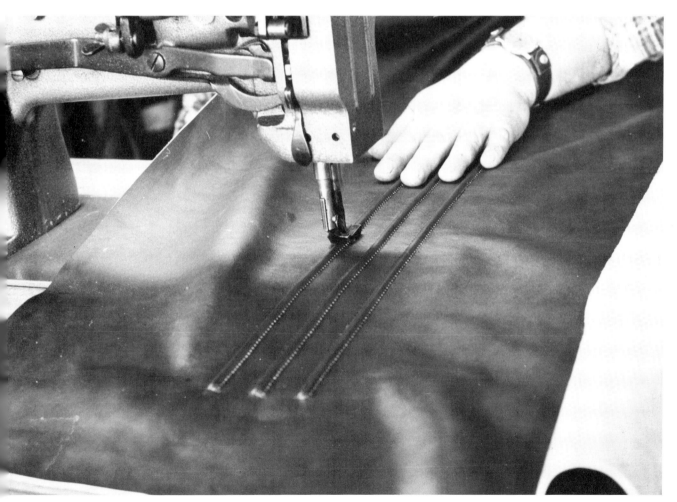

Using the welt foot attachment, he sewed around each strip of cord. Start and end near the middle to make uniform stitches all around and hide the start-stop point.

ed by buttons depressing the cover into a padded backing. On a side wall this lightly padded cover is applied directly to the panel board. On seats it installs over another, thicker layer of padding.

Lay the cover material face up over a piece of cloth-backed foam of the desired thickness. Draw the design and also the top-to-bottom and side-to-side center reference lines from your pattern onto the cover. Allow several extra inches of material on all sides.

For side wall panels, lay out the design on the panel board and drill a 1/4in hole at each button location. Lay the cover with foam backing over the board, line up the design, and punch a hole through the cover and backing at each button point with an awl. Insert buttons with prongs into the holes and bend the prongs over the back side. If the tufted pattern extends to the edges of the panel, pull the cover over the edges and glue and/or staple it to the back side.

If the tufted surface design is for a seat cover, the buttons may tie through a thicker layer of padding. One way to do this is to cut the chosen padding—foam, Dacron, or cotton—of the desired thickness to the size and shape of the seat surface. Glue the padding to a piece of heavy material such as canvas or denim. Position the cover on the padding and hold it in place with upholsterer's pins. Pierce the cover, padding, and backing with an awl at each button location. Use eyelet buttons and twine to tie them in. With a needle, pull the twine through all the layers, and tie the end through an old shirt button or around a wad of cotton or Dacron to prevent it from pulling out. When all buttons are in place, tighten them all to a uniform, desired height. The section on buttons, below, tells how to tie a figure-eight knot that can be adjusted.

Topstitched Designs

Some button tuft designs, like some tuck-and-roll designs, are sewn into the cover for greater definition. If that was the case with your original upholstery, draw the design onto the face of the cover material and place it over a sheet of 1/4 or 1/2in cloth-backed foam or other padding. Then sew the cover and backing together along each line, first those running in one direction, then those going the other way.

If the cover requires puffier tufts or more definition, use foam of the desired thickness, but slit it along the design lines to 1/4in from the backing cloth (don't cut all the way through). Tuck the cover material down into the slits, pinning it in place if necessary, then hold the slits open as you sew along the lines. Punch holes and add buttons as described above.

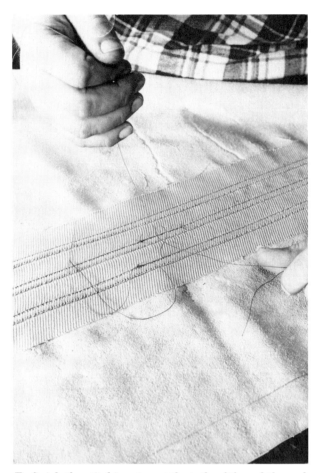

To finish the stitching, insert the tails of thread through the eye of a needle and pull them through to the back side and tie the tails off in back to prevent them from pulling loose.

Making a Tufted Panel

Button tufting often provides more definition to a panel's design. A puffier motif can be created by cutting holes through a block of foam the desired thickness with a punch or a sharpened piece of tubing. The buttons and the cover material are then tucked down into the holes and the buttons secured to a backing. Make a fold in the cover material between each pair of buttons, and the pressure of the compressed foam will maintain the fold. The foam can also be sliced part way through along the pattern lines, leaving at least 1/4in uncut, and the cover material tucked into the slit.

When making a seat cover, construct the button tufted panel with a heavy fabric backing such as denim or canvas. The entire panel is then sewn to other panels as required to complete the seat cover, or applied directly to the seat frame. For an early roadster or touring car where the original seats are missing, you can construct button tufted cushions directly on a

To make windlacing, cut a strip of the cover material about four inches wide, two inches for welt cord. Apply adhesive to the length of rubber windlace core and evenly to the back of the cover material. Allow it to become tacky. Fold the material over for a smooth finish on the end. Place the windlace core in the center of the strip and wrap the material around it.

frame cut from 1/2in plywood to fit the interior. Cut additional foam to provide the needed cushion height and glue it to the plywood platform. Glue the tufted cushion to the foam platform, and finish by stretching the cover over the edges and stapling.

For a curved seat back, make a template or pattern of heavy paper or cardboard of the area to be covered, and transfer it to a piece of 3/16in plywood. By applying steam or soaking the plywood in a hot tub, you can bend it to the desired contour.

Unless you have an example to go by, start with two inches of medium- to high-density foam for padding the backrests, two to four inches for the cushion in addition to the two inches used to create the cover. Add more padding as necessary until the seat height and fullness look right.

To construct a tufted cover directly on the plywood platform, lay out the tuft design on the plywood, mark the button locations and drill a

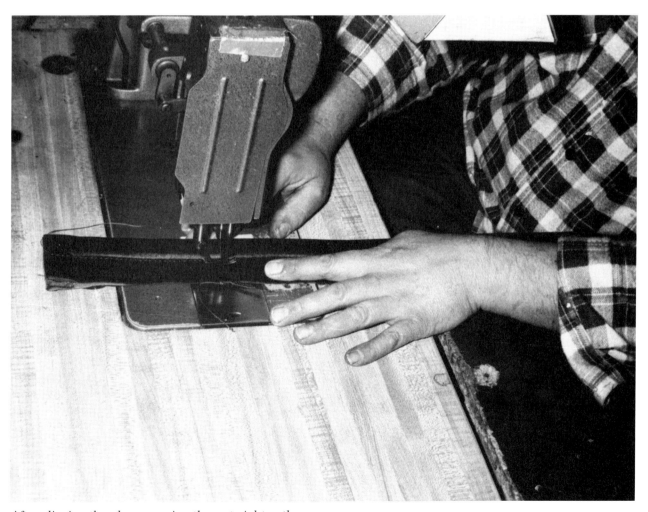

After aligning the edges, pressing the material together, and tucking it firmly against the core, stitch the windlacing close to the core with a welt foot.

1/4in hole at each point. Transfer the button tuft design to a two inch piece of foam and the cover material . Punch holes through the foam at button locations. Proceed with the tufting directly onto the plywood form, inserting the button ties through the holes in the foam and plywood and tying them to washers on the back. Pull the cover material over the edges and staple it securely.

Begin stapling at the center and work outward. Pull the cover into position at intervals of a few inches and staple it temporarily. When it is straight and as tight as desired, go back and staple the edge at 1/2in intervals. Trim the material 1/2in from the staple line. If pleats between buttons are to continue over the edge, fold them into the material, align them with the buttons and staple in place.

On a roadster or touring car, it may be that the tufted seat cover rolls over the edge of the body and attaches to a tack strip on the outside. In this case, extra padding is inserted to build up a roll at the top of the backrest. A decorative or finishing strip such as hide-em is then installed to hide the staples.

Sewn Pleats with Tufts

Sometimes a tufted upholstery design was created by sewing pleats into the cover between buttons. This creates distinct tufts with less fabric and eliminates the need to hand form each pleat. This type of cover is usually made with a layer of padding one inch thick or so, which is slit part way through to allow the cover to pull down.

To incorporate 1/4in pleats between buttons, adjust the measurements of the layout you draw onto the back of the cover material by 1/2in per button from the pattern put onto the foam and backing.

Fold the cover, back side out, on each pattern line and sew 1/4in inside the fold. Some trimmers sew in an arc between each pair of buttons, which creates more of a pocket for the button. First, sew all the pleats in one direction, that is, parallel with each other. Then go back and sew the pleats across in the opposite direction.

Punch holes for the buttons just beside each intersection. Be consistent in putting the holes in the same position relative to the seam, but be careful not to cut the thread. The cover and buttons can now be installed with padding and backing as before.

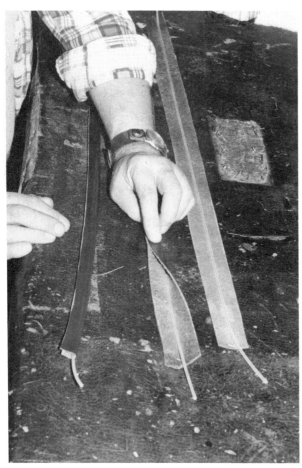

Welt cord is made with a narrower strip of material and plastic core.

Trim the core at an angle back one to two inches from the end of the strip.

Tufting Without Buttons

You may run across upholstery finished with a button tufted effect, but without buttons. In this case, tucks are taken in the material and pulled down where the buttons would be.

Prepare the cover as described above for sewn pleats. Instead of sewing the pleats continuously, leave a gap of 1/4in to 1/2in at each button point. Then insert and tie a piece of twine at each of these points. Depending upon the fabric, you may need to glue a square of canvas to the back so the twine won't pull through the material. With a needle, insert the twine through the padding and backing, and tie it to a shirt button or wad of cotton on the back side. You now have a tuck in the cover, but without a button.

Buttons

Buttons may be used in various ways, beyond button tufting. Sometimes their role is solely for decoration, but they are usually used to pull the cover down into the padding to create an undulating surface. Buttons create many different designs and three-dimensional effects in upholstery.

The types of buttons were mentioned briefly in chapter five but need to be discussed here in a bit more depth. If you cannot get pre-finished buttons that are correct for your job, and you don't wish to invest in a button-making machine, consider taking your buttons and a piece of cover material to an upholstery shop to have them made up.

Seats and heavily padded pieces use a button with an eyelet on the back. A length of button twine is tied to it, inserted through the fabric and padding, and tied to the seat frame or secured to the backing with a wad of cotton or a large shirt or coat button to keep it from pulling out. Your car may have some other arrangement for tying buttons.

To tie twine to the button so it will slip as it is tightened, first put the twine around one side of the eyelet, then put both ends through the eyelet from the other side. To make an upholsterer's figure-eight knot that can be tightened to pull the buttons down to a uniform depth, take one strand of twine in each hand. Hold the left one straight. Loop the right strand under the left, then back over both, under and around both, and finally through the first loop. When the left strand is pulled, the right can slide up, pulling the button tighter. When tightened to the desired position, tie an overhand knot to hold the figure-eight knot in place.

Pillow Backs

A seat upholstery style that drifted over to automobiles from the furniture industry in the seventies is the pillow back or pillow cushion. As the name implies, it consists of a padded element constructed like a pillow, enclosed on three or four sides, and attached to the back or cushion of the seat. Besides heightening the luxury look, it adds some padding and gives the rider somewhat of a floating feeling.

The pillow back is rather complicated to construct and requires a lot of patience. Experience is also a big plus. Since welting is usually involved, be sure the machine you're using can handle several layers of material.

The pillow itself consists of a front panel and three pieces joined together to form a partial back or rim. A thicker pillow may have two additional side panels and a top panel. The partial back panels are joined to the top and side bolsters of the seat cover, which are in turn joined to the back to complete the cover. This type of seat often involves different types of material, for instance, a velour face with vinyl sides and back.

Draw the outline of the pillow face panel onto the cover material and cut it out with a couple inches on all sides for seaming. Cut a matching piece of 1/2in cloth-backed foam and sew the cover material to it around the marked edge. Trim the edge 1/4in outside the seam.

In the same manner, trace from your patterns the pieces that form the rim of the pillow. Cut them out, sew them to 1/4in foam and trim just outside the seam. Measure and mark the top piece where the seams should fall at the corners when the side pieces are sewn to it. Sew the top and two side pieces together; place them face to face and sew on the back side for a blind stitch. Next, sew a welt along the full length of this piece on the edge that will attach to the facing.

Measure and mark the center point of the top edge of both the face and rim, and make alignment marks on both parts at several other points. With the two pieces face to face, begin at the top center point and sew around in one direction, joining the rim and facing with the welt between. Check for equal stretching at each alignment point. After reaching the end, start at the center again and sew around the other side. Finish by cutting a piece of muslin or similar material the size of the pillow and sewing it to the back to form a sack to contain the pillow's foam padding.

Set the completed pillow aside and construct the rest of the seat cover. It consists of a top, two side bolsters, and an outside back panel. These pieces form a horseshoe that encloses the pillow. Draw these elements from your patterns onto the cover material and cut them out. Depending upon how the seat is padded, these panels may or may not require padded backing. If it is molded foam, as shown in the photos, no backing is necessary. Otherwise you may wish to add a backing of 1/4in or 1/2in cloth-backed foam to give the cover a smooth finish.

Join these three panels with blind-stitched seams. Add welts to the seams if that was done

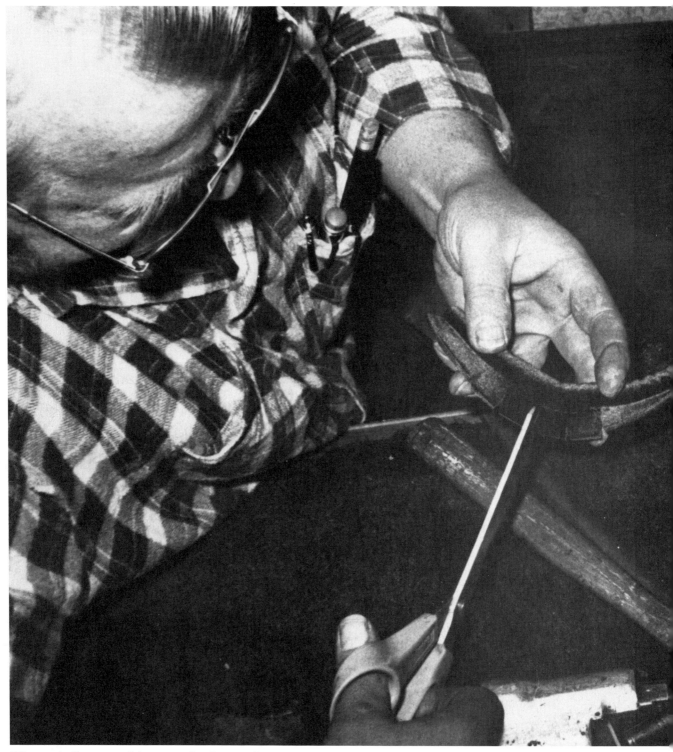

Where windlace or welting must bend around corners, make cuts nearly through the attachment flap at about 1/2in intervals to allow it to curve smoothly.

originally; it adds strength to the seam. Sew welting around the edge that joins the back panel. Sew the top panel and side panels to the back panel to form the horseshoe. The original probably had

welting around the opening that attaches to the pillow section, so add it now.

The back horseshoe-shaped section and the front pillow section must be placed face to face, or

Again using your pattern for the pillow face, trace the outline onto a piece of foam the desired thickness as determined by the original, and cut it out. Insert the foam padding into the sack you sewed into the back of the pillow. When it is situated correctly with no folds or bulges, hog-ring the sack opening shut.

Pillow seat cushions are often decorated with buttons or other ornaments, which also helps hold the foam in place. Install them at this point. Mark the locations on the face of the pillow—they should be indicated on your pattern. With an awl, pierce holes for inserting the buttons, taking precautions to avoid piercing through the back panel. Insert and secure the buttons, and your pillow-cushion cover is ready to install on the seat.

Other Designs

An infinite variety of designs were incorporated in auto and truck interiors; effects created by combinations of padding, pleats, stitching, buttons, and other ornaments and bright trim. Study those used in your vehicle's interior carefully for clues on how to duplicate those effects. Make notes on the pieces you remove or the patterns you draw as to the direction the piece lies, ornaments, edge welting, etc. Following are some techniques you may have to master to complete your interior.

Stitched Designs

Some designs are topstitched directly into the cover material. The pattern or design is transferred to the face of the material. Cut a piece of 1/4in cloth-backed foam large enough to encompass the design area plus a few inches on all sides. Align the cover and the foam and glue together with contact cement. Sew in the design by stitching along the pattern lines drawn on the cover. The machine will sew through the padding to give it the desired sculptured look.

If more definition is required, use a thicker foam. Some designs were merely stitched into the cover without the padded backing, possibly with thread of a contrasting color.

Welt Cord

Another method of defining lines is with welt cord. Welt cord comes in various sizes, and the outline will be raised from the surrounding surface by about half the thickness of the cord.

Draw the design pattern onto the back side of the cover with chalk or pencil. Glue the welt cord to the material along the design lines. The original may have been finished by just stretching and gluing the cover over the cord, or it may have been sewn for better definition.

After trimming the ends of the welt cord to the

inside out. Again marking the top center and working from that point, sew the sections together in one direction, then in the other. Turn the finished cover right side out.

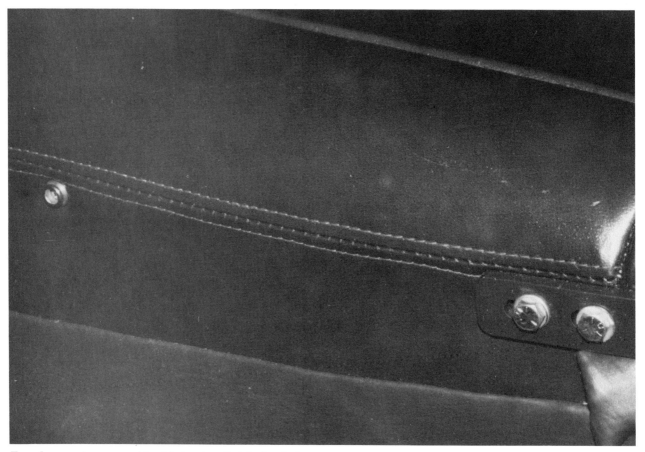

French seam is common for joining two finished uphol-stery panels.

correct point, cut a piece of fabric—any scrap with a tight weave that will hold the stitches—and glue it over the welt cord. On the front side, press the cover tightly against the welt to make a well-defined line. Stitch tightly against the edge of the welt with the welt foot on the machine. Begin sewing somewhere in the middle on the bottom side of the design, if there is a bottom, and sew all the way around, ending up where you began. Finish by sticking the tails of the thread through to the back side and tying them. There will be no tails or loose ends showing on the outside, and the beginning and ending point will be at the least visible spot.

Cardboard

Another approach is to cut cardboard—the type and weight used for cereal boxes, for example—to define a design. Draw the panel's entire design onto the back of the cover. Cut out your cardboard design and glue it into position on the back of the fabric. Glue a piece of backing cloth over the cardboard as outlined for welt cord. Turn the material face up, and press it tightly around the cardboard to define the design lines. If stitching is called for, sew around the cardboard outline as instructed for welt cord.

Sculpturing

You may encounter sculptured panels on some later model cars. As usual, you will need to study the construction of the original and figure out how to repair or duplicate it. In some cases damaged sections of foam can be cut away and new foam cut and glued into place to duplicate the shape of the original.

Raised or depressed panels can be created by layering foam. For a raised section, cut 1/4in, high-density foam to the required shape (add more layers if needed to raise the section more) and glue it to the panel. For a sunken design, cover the rest of the panel with foam and cut out the sunken areas. Then, as you glue on the cover material, press it down tightly around the raised or depressed sections to form a distinct edge.

Occasionally a design might call for a separate insert which attaches to the cover or fits into a depressed section of the panel. These can be created by cutting Masonite or panel board to the desired shape and attaching screws or clips as necessary for attachment. Cover the piece with a light layer of foam padding and the cover fabric, then attach it to the panel.

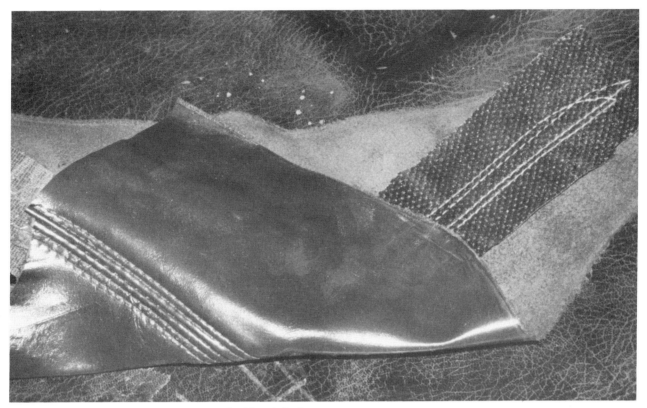

French seam on a leather seat cover is double-stitched for additional strength. Note the heavy fabric reinforcement on the back.

Making Welting and Windlacing

Ready-to-install vinyl or plastic welting and fabric windlacing in a wide variety of colors are available from antique auto upholstery suppliers. However, if they don't have exactly what you need, you can make your own welting or windlace.

Here's where you can use the long, narrow scraps of cover material left over from cutting out other parts. You'll need strips 1-1/2in wide to make welt cord, four inches wide for windlace. Plastic welt core comes in sizes 3/32 to 5/32in. Rubber windlace core is 1/2in in diameter (1/2in rubber vacuum hose from an auto supply store can be used).

Measure to determine the length of cord you need. There's a good possibility you'll have to splice material together to make a long enough continuous piece. For vinyl or cloth, cut the ends at a forty-five degree angle, place the two strips face to face with the ends aligned and sew together. The seam will be barely visible.

If joining two strips of leather, trim the ends straight across. Then, with a razor blade, cut the end of one strip with a forty-five-degree taper in the top edge and the adjoining strip with a matching taper on the bottom edge. Join the edges with Elmer's Craft Bond or a similar glue. One strip overlaps the other slightly to provide an adequate

bonding surface. Tap the seam lightly with a smooth hammer to level it out, and it will be almost invisible.

Apply trim adhesive to the back side of the fabric strip, and allow it to set up until tacky. Lay the welt core or windlace core in the center of the strip, fold the fabric over the core, line up the edges and press together firmly and snugly around the core. If you have a sewing machine with a welt foot, sew close to the core.

Seams

Instructions on how to sew would require an entire book in itself. In fact, I'm sure you can find one at the library if you want to develop more sewing skills. As I mentioned earlier, certain facets of upholstery restoration are virtually impossible to accomplish without sewing.

When sewing is mentioned, it will be without specific directions, assuming that you already know how to sew, intend to learn, or are going to farm out the sewing to someone who knows how.

Before proceeding to talk about joining panels together, which can require sewing, I will briefly discuss three basic types of seams found in upholstery work so you'll be familiar with them when they're mentioned elsewhere.

Straight Seam or Blind Seam

This seam is formed by placing two pieces of material face to face and lining up the edges, then sewing parallel to and about 1/4 inch from the edge. When the two pieces are turned face out, the stitching is not visible. This type of seam has the strength of only one row of stitches, and if material is heavy or bulky, it may not lie flat at the seam. For extra strength, a second, reinforcing seam next to the first at an interval of 1/16 to 1/8in is recommended.

Flat Felled

This seam is like the straight seam but with a second, visible row of stitches to add strength and make the material lie flat. The first seam is a straight seam as described above. Then the top piece of material is folded over, face up, and another line of stitches is run on the outside and through the joined portion parallel to the first seam. While the flat felled seam lies down flatter than a straight seam, the visible set of stitches may not be desired.

French

Because it is sewn with an additional piece of material behind, the French seam is very strong and is good on the edges of seat covers and other places where there is a lot of stress. Join the two pieces of material first with a straight seam placed 1/2in from the edge instead of 1/4in. Spread out the joined pieces of material face down, fold back the edges on either side of the seam and lay a strip of heavy, woven cloth over the seam. You may want to glue it to hold it in place. Turn the material face up, sew 1/8in on one side and parallel with the seam then 1/8in on the other side. These stitches will be visible, so be very careful to get them straight. Practice with some scrap material until you can do it well. Notice where French seams are used on your original upholstery. They hold well and look great when done correctly.

Joining Panels

While you may be working with only a single piece of material at any one time, several situations call for joining two pieces of material together. If one cut of material doesn't cover a wide area, another piece will have to be added; two different colors or types of material may need to be joined or a border must be mated to a pleated or tufted panel.

Take note of the ways adjoining pieces are held together as you dismantle the original interior. Then do your best to duplicate the techniques as you prepare and install your new upholstery. The seams described above and instructions on inserting welting in the seam should cover most instances.

On rigid side wall panels, covering can be glued and stapled rather than sewn. Sometimes stainless trim will cover a seam where pieces of material join. In such a case, glue the pieces down and trim so they butt together just at the center of the trim attachment holes, or one piece can overlap the other as long as the edge will be covered by the trim.

To form a neat transition line without trim, glue one piece down and mark where the edge of the second piece falls. Lay the second piece upside down on the first, and line up the edges. Locate and mark the juncture line on the back of the top piece. Lay a 1/4inch strip of cardboard along this line and staple along it. When the material is turned face out and glued down, the cardboard will give the joined edge a smooth finish.

Carpet Trim

Adding carpet to the bottom of door and quarter panels is a popular and practical modern practice. It provides a different texture and also protects an area that's subject to scuffing when entering or exiting.

When attaching carpeting to another material, first trim the pile from the edge with a pair of shears (an old electric hair clipper works fine, too). The result will be a well-defined line that's easier to follow and prevents the carpet pile from being sewn down and leaving an irregular edge.

The carpet panel usually has an edging of matching or contrasting vinyl or fabric. Cut a strip about two inches wide. Mark the center of the strip, lengthwise, and also the center of the carpet panel. Lay the carpet pile side up and the edging strip upside down on top of it. Line up the center marks and align the edge. Begin in the center and sew together 1/4in from the edge in one direction. Then return to the center and sew out in the other direction. The two types of material don't stretch at the same rate, so sewing from the center out will keep them even, and the ends can be trimmed.

Turn the edging strip face out and pull around the edge of the carpet. On the pile side of the carpet, sew along slightly in from the fold of the edging of strip to attach the edging strip to the back of the carpet. Separating the pile with your fingers as it goes through the machine will hide the stitches.

The edging strip may serve to attach the carpet piece to the panel board. In this case, glue the carpet panel in place. Then pull the edging over the edge of the panel board and glue or staple it to form a neat, finished edge.

Carpeting may also serve as filler for character lines in the fabric. To accomplish this, lay the fabric face down on the carpet with the edge as far back from the carpet edge as necessary to add the design lines. Sew the fabric to the carpet. Apply adhesive to both the fabric and the carpet, fold the fabric face out, and press it down to adhere to the carpet. Draw the lines onto the fabric with chalk, and topstitch along the lines. The carpet pile will fill between the stitched lines to give them definition.

Chapter Seven

Upholstering Seats

Are there seats in your project car? Good. You've got a place to start! If they're still wearing at least some of the original covering, you even have material samples to match when buying new fabric.

If seats are missing, check around the salvage yards and swap meets to find some that are serviceable. New replacement seat units are available for Model A Fords and some other popular models. Suppliers also offer seat springs and other parts separately to repair and rebuild seats. This is the time to change seats if you've contemplated, for example, switching to bucket seats or upgrading to a seat with a fold-down center armrest.

Making a Pattern

Carefully remove the original seat cover and identify each piece. Then take the cover apart and use the individual pieces as patterns for cutting new material. Always be sure to allow at least 1/2in for sewing seams.

In the event there's no cover to go by, make a pattern out of a cheap, non-stretch material like muslin or duck. Secure the desired amount of padding over the springs, then fit the muslin to the seat. Once it fits as desired, cut it apart and use the pieces to lay out and cut the cover material. This will save time in the long run and lower the risk of ruining an expensive piece of material.

Make a Fitting Dummy

Another approach is to leave the covering on the seat and use it as a dummy to help you measure, sew, and fit the new covers, provided the cover is fairly intact and the correct design. Measure and mark the center line of each section with chalk as a reference point. It may be helpful to also draw a model of the seat cover with all its components. If more than one kind of material is involved, indicate which parts are of what fabric. Measure on your dummy where the various panels join. Write these measurements on your model for later reference, and if it's convenient, also write them on the old cover. When cutting and sewing panels to construct the new seat cover, check the fit frequently against the original.

Constructing the Seat Cover

For the sake of illustration, let's consider a roll-and-pleat seat cover. This one, in burgundy leather, is for a 1949 Hudson convertible. The roll-

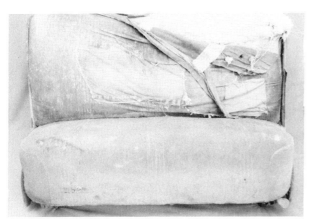
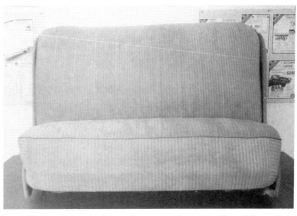

Above and right, a presewn reupholstery kit from Kanter Auto Products turned the patched and frayed relic at left into the like-new seat on the right. Corduroy, broadcloth, mohair, velour and vinyl materials are offered in original styles.

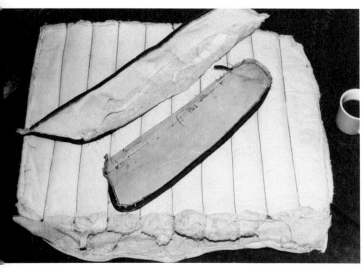

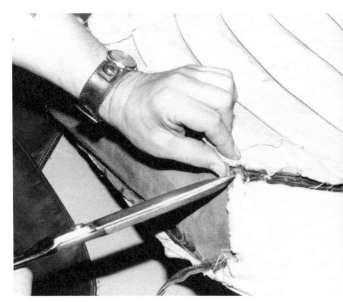

When dismantling the original seat cover, separate the individual parts of one side (driver's or passenger's) to use as patterns while leaving the other side together to show how it is assembled and sewn together. If that's not possible, draw yourself a picture.

As he removes the seat bolster, Norm Kyhn cuts a notch to show where the side panel lines up with the welt. Do this wherever there's an identifiable juncture.

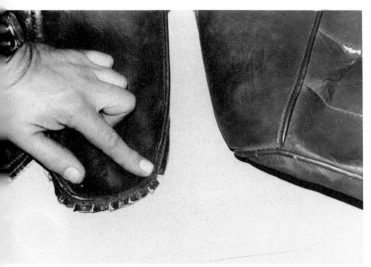

Notch will be transferred to the new material to make it easier to line up as the new cover is constructed.

and-pleat sections run to the edge of both the cushion and the split backrest; other designs might have a horseshoe of plain material around a pleated insert.

The driver's side backrest in this example was left intact to serve as a guide, while the passenger backrest was taken apart and the individual panels used as patterns. You'll do well to follow the same procedure. Mark or cut notches to indicate junctures where one panel must line up with a seam or welt on another panel.

Lay the patterns on the new cover material and outline them with chalk. With leather you

Chalk the pattern for the main section of the backrest cover onto the tuck-and-roll panel constructed in Chapter Six. Line up the bottom edge and the outside pleats.

may have to try several arrangements to make the best use of the hide's irregular shape. Lay out the larger panels first on the best part of the hide. You don't want holes or scars showing in obvious places like the seat surface, so work around them; if possible, place blemishes where they can be trimmed and discarded entirely, or try to put them out of sight, such as on an edge that will be turned un-

Stitch just inside the chalk line all around the perimeter. Be sure all pleats are lying the same direction. Sewing will secure them permanently that way.

One edge of the vinyl tail is marked to line up with pleats of the bottom of the seat back panel. Make a mark one and a half inches from the opposite edge, lay a length of plastic welt cord in this space, then fold the edge over to the line and sew the welt cord into the envelope. This forms a strong edge to attach to the seat.

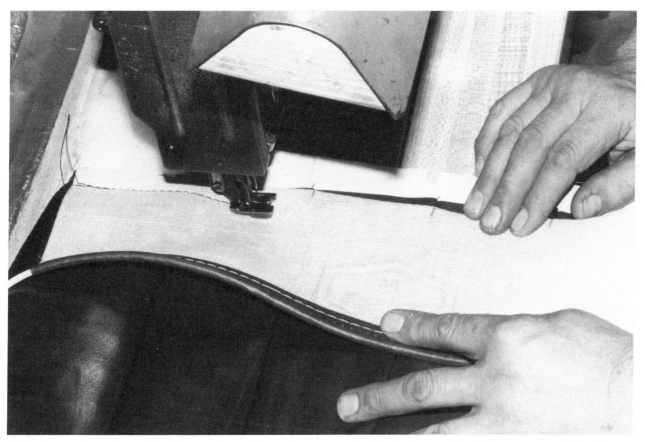

With the two pieces face to face, line up the marks on the tail with the pleats of the cover, and align the edge of the tail with the bottom edge of the cover panel. Sew the two pieces together 1/2in from the edge.

Cut out the top and side pieces for the backrest cover individually and glue them to scrim.

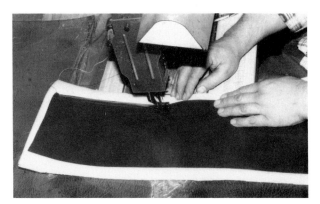

Perimeter-sew the leather cover to the scrim and trim the scrim even with the edge of the leather.

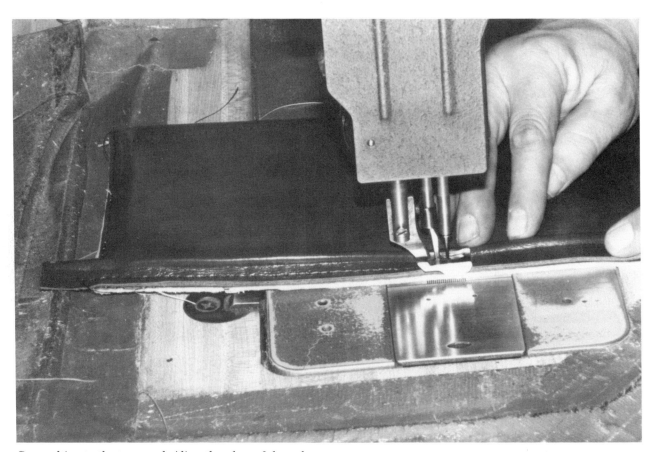

Sew welting to the top panel. Align the edges of the welt and the panel and sew 1/4in from the edge.

der. Be sure to transfer any of the marks you made to indicate seam or welt locations.

If you're doing two identical or mirror-image pieces, like right and left backrests, lay out both on the material, but cut out and assemble only one. If it's not quite right, you've only ruined one piece!

Make up the tuck-and-roll (or other design) main panel as described in Chapter Six, but don't stuff the rolls just yet; that makes it too hard to work with.

Lay it out on your work table. Lay your pattern over the cover panel, outline it in chalk, and stitch around just inside the chalk line. For a professional look, it's important that all the pleats face the same direction; those on the seats should all lie either to the left or right and those on the side walls to the front or rear, top or bottom. When you sew around the perimeter, you're setting them permanently. Cut out the panel about 1/16in outside the stitch line.

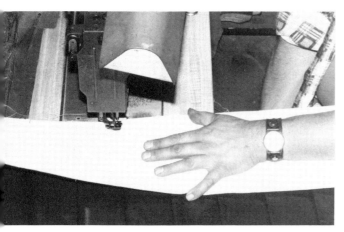

Mark three-inch intervals on the edge of the top panel that will join the pleated panel. Place the top panel face to face with the top edge of the pleated panel, with the welt between. Align the edges, and sew the panels together with the welt foot. Place the seam snug against the welt cord.

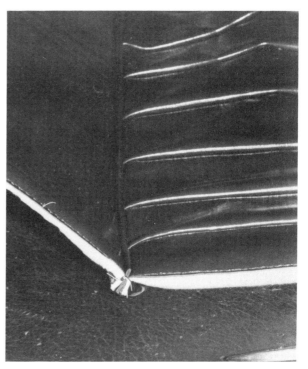

This is how the seam should look with the welt sandwiched between two panels.

Most seat covers have a tail at the back of the cushion or bottom of the backrest for attaching to the frame. Cut this panel out of vinyl or other heavy material, and mark one edge in intervals corresponding with the pleats on the cover. Fold the opposite edge over a welt cord and sew the cord in. Place the tail and cover face to face, line up the edges and align the marks with the cover pleats. Sew together 1/2in from the edge. Besides attaching the tail, this will control the width of the pleats.

Individually cut out the other pieces that make up the cover, and glue them to scrim (muslin-backed 1/2in foam). Perimeter sew the scrim and cover material together 1/8–1/16inch from the edge and trim the scrim. Most seat cover construction calls for welting between the face and side panels. If the welt cord can be separated from the cover, cut the cord back 1 to 1-1/2in from the end and place that point 1/2in inside the edge of the panel. Line up the edges and sew the welt and the panel together 1/4in from the edge. Make marks on the edge of the top panel to align with the pleats on the face panel. Place the two panels face to face with the welt sandwiched between, align the edges and sew together using a welt foot to place the seam next to the cord.

Attach the other panels in the same manner. Especially on seats, which can be subjected to considerable stress, you may want to reinforce the seams by sewing a second seam parallel to and 1/8–1/16in from the first. At panel edges, open the welt and sew across. This will make the welt lie down smoother. Where welt must follow a curve, make slits at 3/8–1/2in intervals to allow it to bend.

If you're making individually stuffed pleats, you should make up the cover to this point before stuffing. Then slit open the pockets in the muslin backing at each end and insert the filling as described in Chapter Six. Finally, sew welting around the entire edge of the finished cover. This welt forms a strong border to attach the cover to the springs with hog rings. It won't show, so it can be made of vinyl or scraps.

Preparing Seat Frames

With all the old covering and padding removed, inspect the seat frame and make necessary repairs. Replace broken or badly sagging springs. Earlier car seats consist of top and bottom frames, usually of heavy wire, with a set of coil springs between. Damaged springs can be replaced individually. Be sure the wires, springs, or—in some cases—cord that tie the springs in place are in good shape and all springs are attached as they should be.

Later models use sinuous, or zigzag, springs made of heavy-gauge steel wire with zigzag bends. Some of them may be stretched by years of use. You can salvage better zigzag or coil springs from another seat or buy new replacements from an upholstery supply house. Check to see that the zigzag springs are properly attached to the frame and that wire clips holding them in line are intact. If the perimeter framework is broken, it can be welded or a new piece cut and attached with collars.

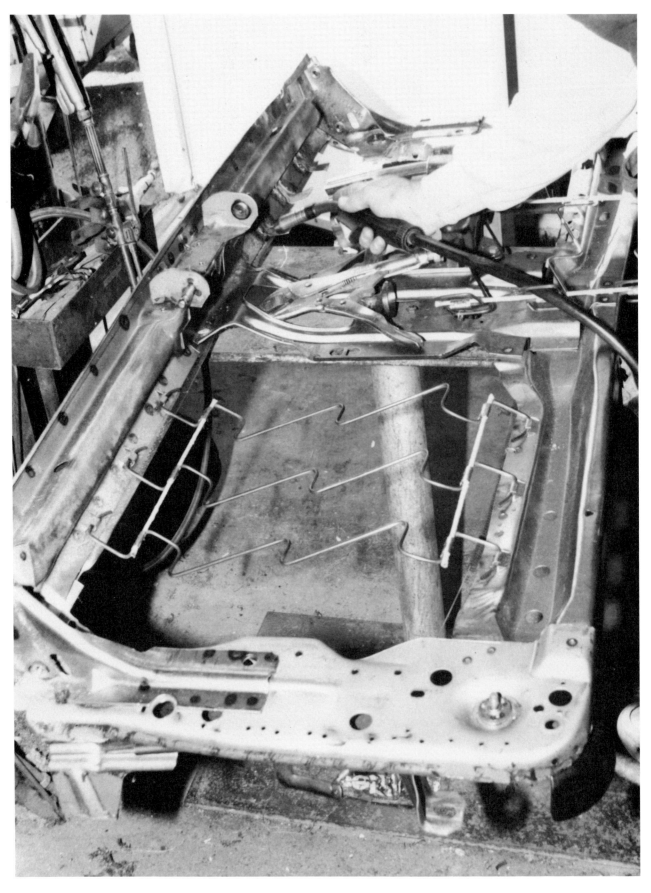

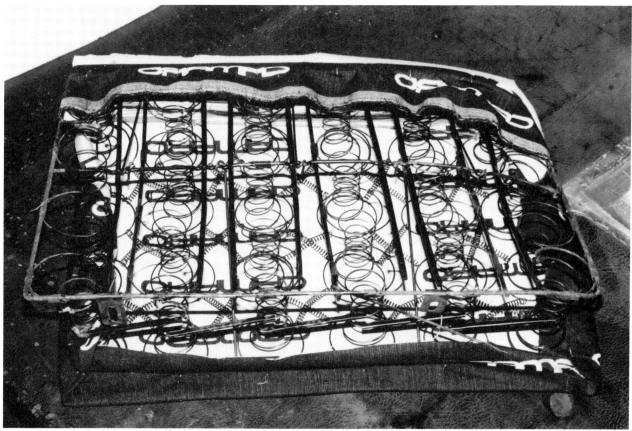

Tough and cheap, burlap was used to cover springs and provide a base for padding. Any heavy, woven material, *such as the left-over Camaro seat cover fabric shown in use here, will work as well.*

A wire brush can be used to remove rust, or you might want to have the frame and springs sand blasted if they are quite rusty. Then refinish them with a rust-inhibiting paint or primer.

Installing Padding

Seat padding in modern cars usually consists of a foam bun molded to the desired seat shape and attached directly to the seat unit. If the cover is torn to expose the foam, chances are the foam has been damaged. Seat foam kits pre-molded to the original contours are offered by several suppliers for the more popular models like pony cars and muscle cars of the sixties and seventies.

It's possible to cut out a damaged section and cement in a new piece of foam cut to shape. Foam that has become compressed with age can be rejuvenated with an application of steam. Since the

Opposite page, chances are the seat frame can remain intact, but check to see that all components are attached and adjustment mechanisms are working. Make any necessary repairs. In the case above, some of the tabs that hold the bottom springs were broken on this late seat frame, so Matt Swanson welded in new ones.

passenger seat usually gets less wear, you might find one in a salvage yard with good foam to replace damaged driver's seat padding. Adding a one-inch layer of a new foam will renew and fill out the cushion.

On an older car you will probably need to replace the layer of burlap over the springs that provides a smooth base for the padding. If you have a surplus of some other heavy, woven material, it can be used in place of burlap. Stretch the new material over the frame, pull it over the edge and secure it with hog rings to the first turn of the coil springs. Don't hog-ring to the perimeter wire because the rings can rub and wear through the cover.

Then add the padding. As mentioned before, you may wish to use cotton batting to be authentic, but synthetic foam or Dacron batting is easier to work with. Some early cars had a sisal pad—a layer of horsehair—under the cotton padding on seat cushions. Denim material may have been used over the cotton to hold it in place on seat backs. Some suppliers offer ready-to-install seat padding with burlap, foam polyskin (foam reinforced with plastic backing for toughness), and cotton padding.

If you use foam padding, fit it to the seat and apply a coat of adhesive to hold it in place.

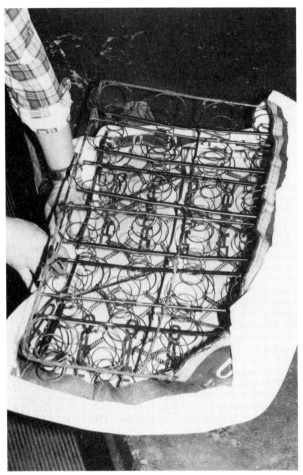

Glue a layer of one-inch foam over the seat spring unit and wrap the foam over the edges.

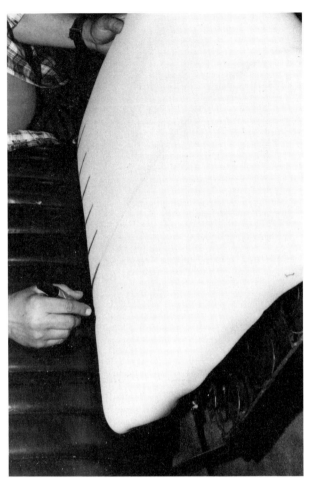

With the newly recovered seat cushion already installed in this Hudson convertible, Norm Kyhn held the back-rest in place and marked the pleat positions on the foam.

Installing the Seat Cover

Turn the cover inside out and work it onto the seat by pulling it right side out. Spraying the surface with silicone helps slide the cover into place. Smaller pieces like armrests can be wrapped in thin plastic to ease sliding the cover on. Work out wrinkles with your hands as you go. Pull and stretch the cover as necessary before securing it in place. An application of steam helps remove wrinkles and makes the cover softer and easier to work into place. Some trimmers use a wand to apply steam between the cover and the padding.

Covering the Seat Back

Our example, the 1949 Hudson convertible, has storage pockets in each front seat back. As with other components, one unit was measured and marked, then disassembled for patterns while the other was left intact for reference.

Cut a piece of panel board to size for the back panel of the pocket, and punch holes for the ends of the elastic pocket opening. Glue the board to a

sheet of vinyl (it is inside, so won't be visible), and trim the vinyl to the edge of the board. Glue muslin to the other side of the board, leaving an edge for sewing.

Cut out the cover material to form the pocket. Fold over the top edge and sew once next to the fold and again about an inch further in to form a sleeve to enclose the elastic. This stitching will be visible, so use thread that matches the cover, sew straight lines, and tie off the ends so they don't pull loose. Insert a screwdriver or other tool into the sleeve so you don't cut both layers as you cut a slit with a razor blade for the elastic.

The original pockets had steel springs, like those on a screen door, which were rusty. A length of bungee cord will work much better. Fabricate ends to hold it to the board. A couple lengths of wire attached with collars made by splitting pieces of tubing is one way.

Pull the elastic through the sleeve with a wire rod. Insert the ends through the holes in the board, bend the wires over on the back side and se-

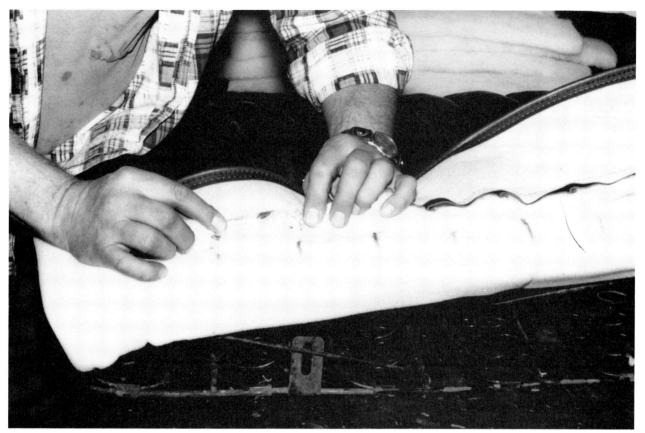

Marks allowed him to line up the pleats of the backrest cover so they'll be in line with those of the cushion when the seat is together.

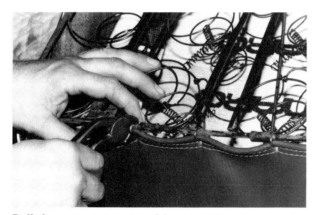

Pull the seat cover taut and hog-ring it to the outer rim of the frame.

Applying steam will also help remove wrinkles and stretch vinyl and leather into finished shape. Spraying lightly with water will also make leather and vinyl more pliable.

cure them with washers and duct tape. Position the pocket on the vinyl-covered panel board and sew around the perimeter. The two sides and the bottom edge will be covered by other panels in this instance.

Cut the side panels according to the patterns and sew them, face down, to the face of the board. Glue a thin layer of padding to the board, fold the side panels over it, and topstitch just inside the edge of the board. The outside panel attaches over this seam. First, stitch on the back side, then fold the material over and run one straight seam close to the fold with cover-color thread. Attach the top and bottom panels in the same manner. If a sewing machine that will sew through

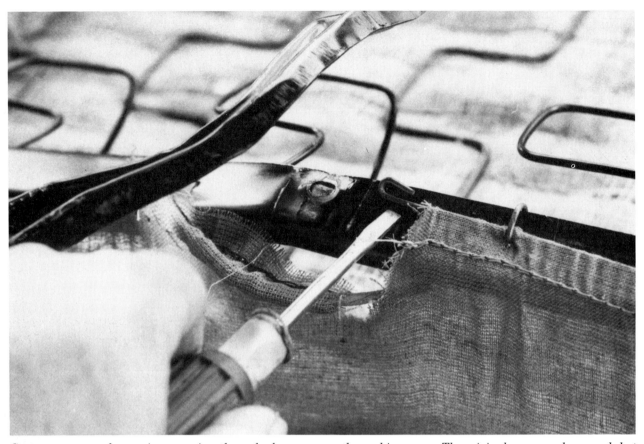

Some seat covers have wires running through sleeves and secured by hog rings to provide uniform tension on the cushion cover. The original ones can be reused, but scuff and paint them so they don't develop rust.

panel board is not available, this construction can be done by stapling, with a strip of cardboard to form a smooth edge, as described in Chapter Six.

Covering the Seat Back

Thoroughly clean the steel seat frame or shell. If needed (they probably will be), attach new tack strips. This can be a strip of Masonite attached with pop rivets. Upholstery panel board can be layered and glued in to follow contours.

Glue a layer of padding to the seat frame and trim it so there's just enough to roll over and pad the edge. Coach wadding used originally is hard to find these days. A good substitute is Dacron padding intended for quilt making. Apply contact cement liberally to both surfaces. Position the upholstered panel, pull the edges snugly over the edge of the seat shell, and staple securely. Take a section at a time, working from the middle outward in each direction. Stretch to eliminate wrinkles as you go, and trim around seat hardware as necessary. Trim the excess material.

Installing Ready-Made Seat Covers

You're in luck if your project is a pony car, a mid-size model from the sixties or early seventies, or one of several other popular models for which complete, ready-to-install seat covers are made. The UPS truck can deliver everything you need to your doorstep within a few days! While you're waiting, you can prepare the seat frame and padding.

The procedure for most cars will be quite similar to the installation shown here on an early Mustang. With the bucket seat backrest separated from the cushion, pry off the back panel with a screwdriver and save the attaching clips. Remove the hog rings to loosen and remove the old cover. Remove the hog rings which hold the wire in the front of the frame. Remove and save the wire encased in the listing strip.

Refurbish or replace the foam bun as necessary.

Turn the new seat cover inside out and thread the wire through the seat listing. Align the cover with the frame and attach it by securing the wire in the cover listing to the inner seat frame wire with the new hog rings. Pull the seat cover over the cushion, right side out. Setting the cover in the sun for a few minutes or carefully applying heat with a hair dryer will make the material more pliable and easier to work with.

Check to see that the cover is lined up correctly on the seat, and work out any wrinkles with

Turn the seat cover inside out and work it over the seat.

This Hudson interior featured pockets on the back of the front seats. One of the original backrests was left intact as a guide while the new assembly for the other side was being made.

Steam applied with a wand between the cover and padding removes wrinkles.

The old cover was marked and measured for determining material requirements.

your hands before turning it over and beginning attachment to the frame with hog rings.

Insert clips into the new seat backrest panel. Reattach the panel by squeezing the clips and inserting them into the corresponding holes in the backrest frame. Follow the same procedure to install the new cover on the seat cushion. Put the back and cushion sections back together, and the seat is ready to go back into the car.

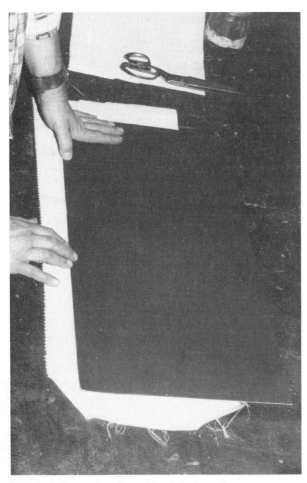

Glue muslin to the other side of the board.

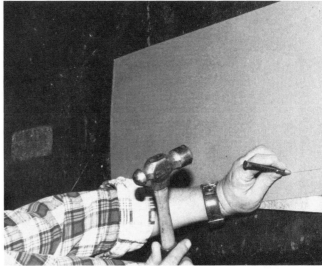

Cut a new panel board to size and punch the holes that will hold the ends of the elastic at the top of the pocket.

Glue the board to a sheet of vinyl, which forms the inside of the pocket, and trim the vinyl to the edge of the board.

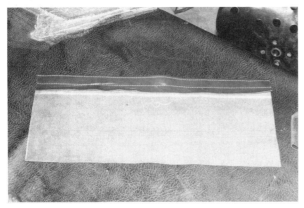

Cut the front of the pocket out of the cover material—leather, in this case. Fold over one edge and sew a sleeve for the elastic to go through.

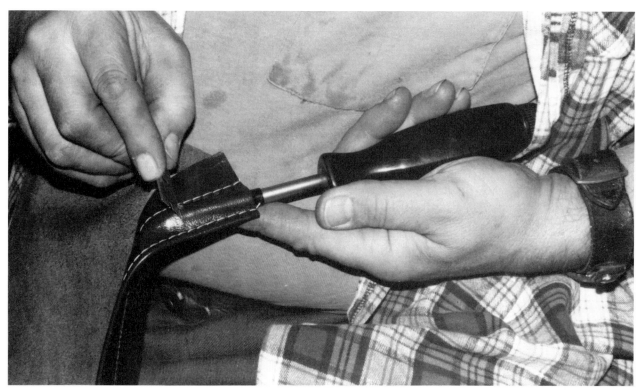

*Insert a screwdriver into the sleeve to prevent cutting
through both layers of material, and use a razor blade to
cut slits for the elastic.*

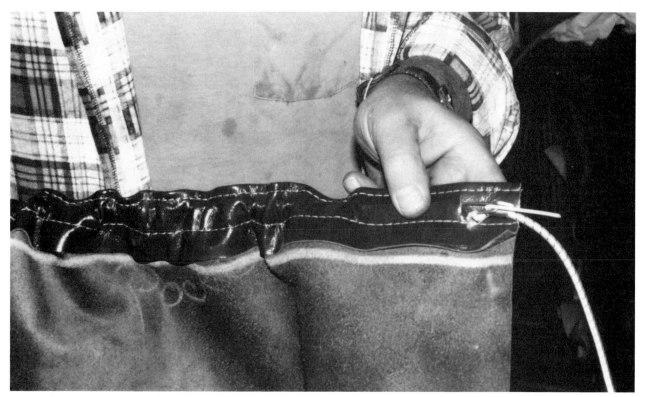

*Use a wire with a crook on the end to pull the elastic—a
bungee cord, in this case—through the sleeve.*

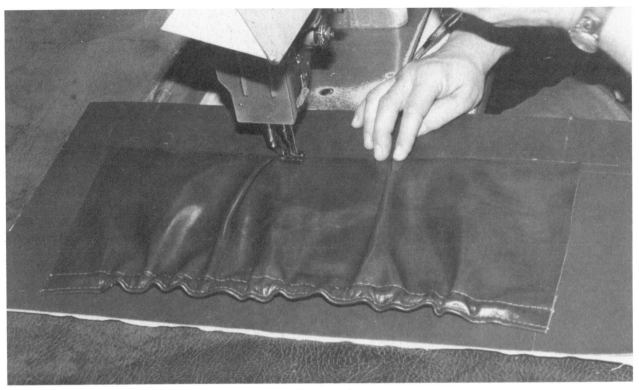

Position the pocket on the board and sew or staple around the perimeter. The edges will be covered by other panels.

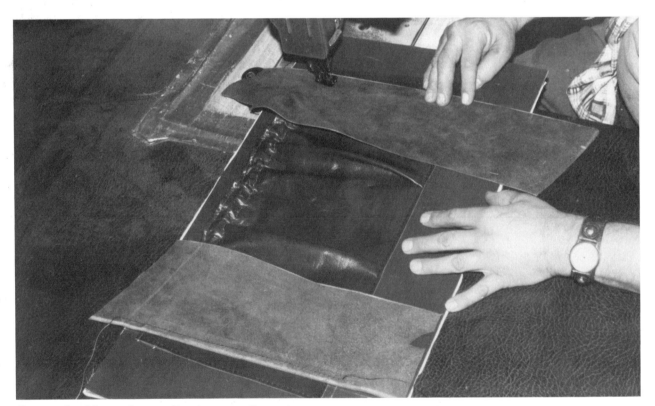

Cut out the side panels according to your patterns, turn them face down and sew one edge to the board even with the pocket edge.

96

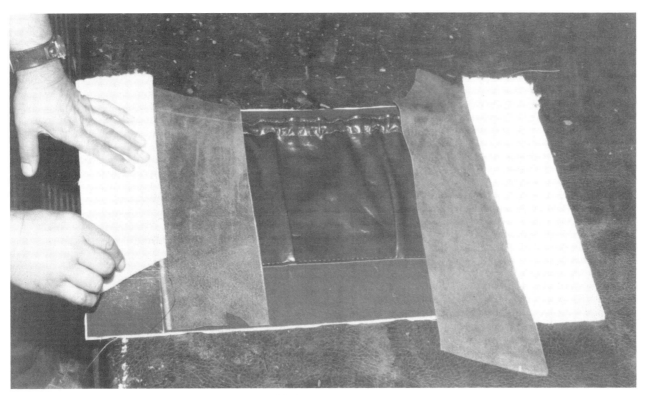

Glue padding to the outer edges of the board. Fold the
side panels over the foam and topstitch it to the board.

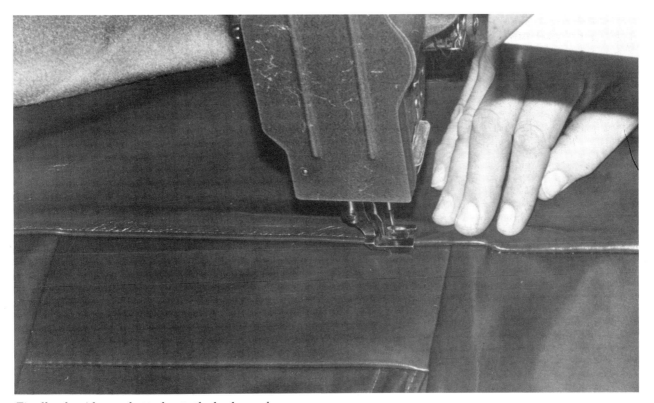

Finally, the side panel attaches to the back panel.

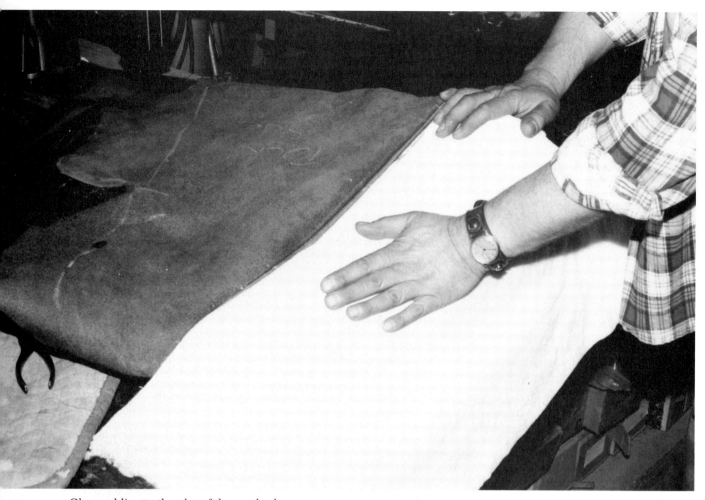

Glue padding to the edge of the seat back.

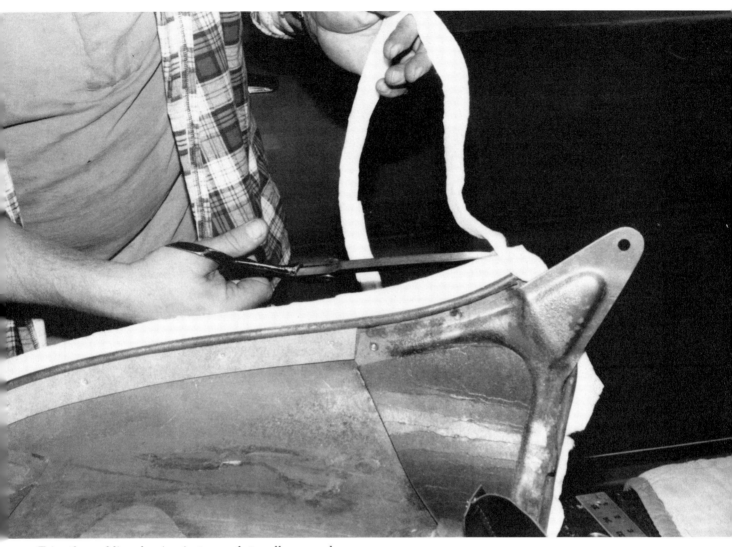

Trim the padding, leaving just enough to roll over and
cushion the edge.

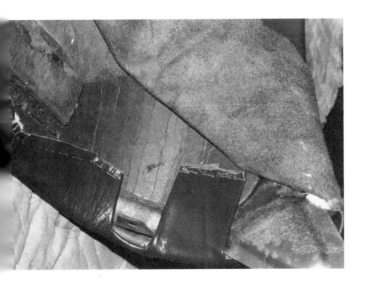

Left, pull the leather cover over the edge and staple it in
place. Two layers of panel board were shaped and glued
into the corner of the seat back to hold staples. Note how
leather cover is formed around the seat bracket.

Above and previous page, with the finished seat covers,
this Hudson interior looks like new.

Chapter Eight

Door and Side Panel Upholstery

The pieces that make up the sides of the passenger compartment are known collectively as the side walls. They consist of the door panels and quarter panels, those behind the front doors of a two-door car or behind the rear doors of a four-door model. The kick panels in front of the front doors extending under the dashboard may also be considered part of the side wall and are upholstered the same way, if they are upholstered at all. So is the center pillar of a four-door sedan.

Being essentially flat, these are probably the easiest upholstered pieces to restore—a good place for the novice to test his or her renovation skills. In many cases, a sewing machine is not necessary; they can be done at home with common hand tools. Experience gained in recovering the side wall panels will help you decide how much of the remainder of the job to tackle yourself.

103

Panel Removal

As in all upholstery operations, take careful note of how panels attach to the body and how the covering is constructed and attached. Usually door handles, window cranks, and armrests have to be removed first. The way they mate with their respective mechanisms and the steel skin helps secure the upholstered panel. The handle may be attached with a screw or Allen-head bolt. If no fastener head is visible, push in on the panel to see how the handle is secured to the shaft. There may be a spring clip that has to be squeezed together with needle-nose pliers or a wire clip requiring a hooked tool or a hook bent into a stiff wire to remove. Some forties and fifties models—Chrysler products come to mind—have a pin that must be forced out with an awl. A few installations require special tools found only in body or trim shops.

Armrests are usually secured with two or more Phillips screws which tap into the steel skin. On some later models you may have to remove an ashtray, hand grip pocket, or trim piece for access to screws that hold the panel on. Remove mirror and power window controls; other hardware and trim items usually attach to the trim panel and can be detached after the panel is out of the car.

Various methods are used to attach side wall panels around the sides and bottom, sometimes more than one on a panel. Remove any visible trim screws or moldings that appear to attach the panel to the body. Most common are spring clips attached to the panel and secured in holes in the metal skin. Carefully insert a putty knife or screwdriver between the panel and the door skin and slide it along until it encounters one of the clips. Twist or carefully pull outward on the tool to work it free. Proceed to the next fastener and repeat the process around the edge of the panel until all clips are loose.

Chevrolets of the fifties, among other models, used a metal strip around the perimeter of the panel with nails which inserted into slots in the door skin. These panels are difficult to remove without breaking, but if you are trying to save them, make a removal tool by grinding a deep notch into the blade of an old screwdriver. Insert the screwdriver behind the panel, slide the notch over the nail and carefully work it loose.

With the panel mostly free, determine how the top is secured. On later models, the metal top of the panel is U-shaped and slips into the window channel and must be lifted upward to clear the channel. On earlier models the window sill and garnish moldings secure the top of the side wall panel. These come off by removing Phillips screws. There might be some clips holding the panel in the middle, requiring that it be slid upward to come free. Time taken to remove side wall panels carefully will be rewarded if the panel can be reused. At any rate, you'll want it as intact as possible to serve as a pattern to make a new one.

Rear quarter panels are secured by similar means. Remove the back seat cushion for access and any handles and garnish moldings. Then you should be able to see any additional fasteners. There will probably be a combination of screws and spring clips. There may also be a tack strip hidden by windlacing to which the upholstered panel attaches. Remove the tacks or staples carefully to avoid damaging the tack strip.

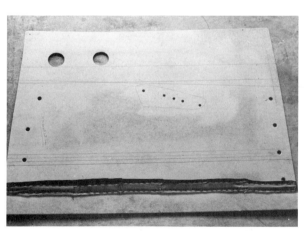

After removing the old door panels, cut new panel board or Masonite to the size and shape of the old panel or the area to be covered. An extra strip is attached to this one with vinyl to extend the depth or make it better fit the curvature of the door. The upholstery design is drawn on the board and holes punched for hardware.

Trace around the old panel onto new panel board, including holes, and then cut out the panel board along the chalk lines. Punch or drill out the trim holes to the correct size. For the larger window crank hole, make the initial hole with a punch and cut to exact size with a utility knife or shears.

With the panel off, remove any hardware attached to it. Trim moldings are usually attached by tabs bent over on the back side or by spring clips. Be careful not to damage the tabs, and straighten them with pliers for re-installation. Inspect the panel board to determine if it's reusable. Often moisture causes it to warp or partially rot away. If that's the case, keep it for a pattern.

Now is a good time to check and clean out drain holes in the bottom of the doors or body panels. When they get plugged up, moisture collects and can not only harm the panel board, but rust the sheet metal, too.

Most cars have a sheet of heavy plastic or paper attached to the door or body skin with adhesive to seal out moisture and dust. If it's in good enough shape to reuse, leave it in place or remove it carefully. If not, save it as a pattern for a new one.

Right and left door and quarter panels will, in nearly all cases, be mirror images of each other. Leave one original intact as a guide as you remove the cover upholstery from the other and separate it into components to serve as patterns.

Panel Construction

Mustangs, Coronets, Camaros, GTOs, Barracudas and many other models have enough of a following that new, reproduction door and side panels are available. In most cases they're upholstered and ready to install. Others may need to be put into position with a couple clips while you mark the locations of door handle and window regulator shafts and armrest screws. You'll probably need to transfer trim moldings from the panel, too. Contact those suppliers listed in the back of the book that carry supplies for your particular model.

Some side wall panels were molded in complex shapes with the cover material bonded on. These require special measures. You may have to repair the ones you have or find used ones in better shape. We discuss these procedures later in this chapter, so if this is your situation, you might want to jump ahead.

If you're starting from scratch, general upholstery supply firms carry panel board for making new door and side panels. The normal thirty-two inch by forty-eight inch size is large enough for

Make up the entire panel cover. Outline marked is the edge of the panel board. An allowance of one to two inches on all sides is left to fold over and staple.

Cut carpet to fit, apply adhesive to both surfaces, then press the carpet onto the panel. Note speaker hole repaired with panel board.

When the outside is secure, turn the panel over and apply cement to the edges of the cover and the panel board. Pull the cover over the edge and glue it down, working from the middle out and stretching the cover as you go. Once it's in place, staple it down and trim the excess.

Moe Wilson made up this new vinyl cover for a door panel, topstitching the pleated pattern over thin padding. After gluing it to the original board, he used a piece of wood and lead weights to press the cover into a depression in the board.

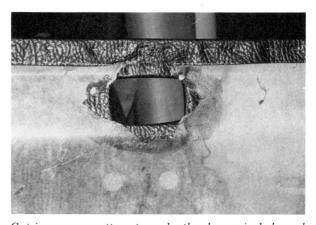

Cut in a cross pattern to make the door grip hole and any other openings. Fold the flaps through the opening and glue them on the back of the panel.

most purposes. Be sure to get waterproof board. Although slightly more expensive, it will hold up better in an automobile. Some trimmers prefer 1/8in thick composition board such as Masonite, or wood wall paneling, both of which offer greater stiffness.

Making a Pattern

Lay the panel board on your work table and trace the outline of the old panel onto it along with locations of all hardware and attachment holes. Cut it out and cut or drill the holes marked.

If neither the panel nor the complete upholstering is usable as a pattern, make one out of a piece of heavy, clear plastic. Secure it over the door with masking tape, then trace the outline 1/8in inside the edge. Mark all holes for hardware and attachment clips. Cut out the pattern and transfer it to the panel board. After cutting the board, sand the edges so they won't wear through the covering.

Hardware and Padding

Hidden spring clips have been the most common means of attaching panels for years, although there have been advances in more recent years. Upholstery suppliers carry them if you need to replace some or switch from another type of attachment. Spring clips usually have a U-shaped portion that grips the panel board and a diamond or Christmas tree-shaped spring portion that fits into the hole in the door skin. They have a 1/2in offset, so the holes in the panel must be offset the same amount from the holes in the door. Try the bare panel for fit on the door and make necessary adjustments before installing upholstery.

The padding will be determined by how it was done on the original panel, or your desire to do it differently. In most cases you will make up the entire panel cover with scrim or foam padding glued or sewn to the back side and install it on the panel board in one piece.

The finished panel exactly matches the original.

This molded fiberboard door panel from a 1965 Thunderbird is deteriorated on the bottom where moisture collects. There is fiber padding or insulation in some areas, and the top is stamped steel.

Remove the stainless trim by prying up tabs bent over on the back side. Avoid damaging the tabs, and straighten them with pliers.

Repair cracked or broken areas. Minor cracks can be covered with wide masking tape.

If it isn't already sewn to the cover, you can glue the padding directly to the panel board. Cut a sheet of 1/4in or 1/2in foam to the size and shape of the panel board. Soft foam can be folded over the edge of the board along with the cover, so cut it to overlap about an inch on all sides. If thicker or firmer material is used, cut it to overlap only enough to form a protective cushion for the fabric around the edge of the board.

When correctly trimmed, position the foam on the board. Hold half of it in place while you fold back the other half, and spray adhesive on both

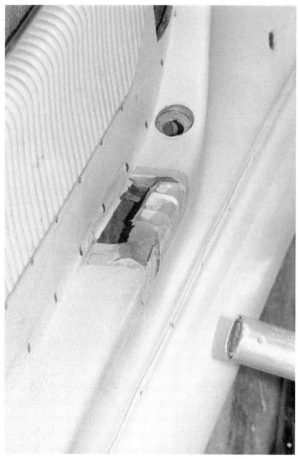

The molded door panel goes to pot in high wear areas like the hand grip. Surface cracks also develop with age. The damage here will be cut and filled to shape with new foam cut and glued in place.

Cut a piece of vinyl to cover the area being repaired. After checking the fit, apply contact cement to the back side and also to the door panel (if spraying, mask off areas where you don't want glue).

the foam and the board. Carefully fold this half into place and press it down. Repeat with the other half. Cut out all trim holes with scissors.

Making the Panel Cover

In Chapter Six we covered most of the techniques necessary to make up side panel upholstery. Whatever elements are involved—pleated or tufted panels, two or more different kinds of colors of material—make up the complete panel using combinations of these techniques. Follow the original methods as closely as possible. Were two pieces of material joined with a blind seam? Turn them face to face and sew so the stitches will be out of sight. Were other seams top-stitched? With one or more rows of stitches? Did the thread match or contrast with the fabric? Was a welt cord sewn into the seam?

Was a design stitched into the panel, such as parallel lines for a pleated look, decorative lines or something more intricate? With chalk or pencil, trace the panel's outline from your pattern onto the face of the cover material, and add horizontal

and vertical center lines for reference. Then draw the design onto the cover. Glue a sheet of scrim—the amount of definition desired in the pattern will determine the thickness—onto the back of the cover. Following the design lines, sew the design into the cover.

Sometimes panel designs are created with two different colors or types of material overlapped and the heat-sealed seam where they join hidden by a stainless molding. As long as the seam will be covered, go ahead and sew the pieces together for strength.

Carpeting is often added along the bottom of a panel for accent and to absorb the soiling and scuffing that occurs in that area. Again, note how it was attached originally and try to duplicate that. If it is sewn to an adjoining panel of another material or has a vinyl binding around the edge, shave the nap from the edge to make sewing easier. The carpet panel may be attached to another panel with a blind stitch or top stitch, stainless steel molding, or glued directly to the sidewall panel.

Lay the new vinyl over the panel. Fold it back and glue down half at a time. Another set of hands may be handy for this task. Press down the flat areas first, then use a *heat gun or hair dryer to make the vinyl more pliable as you form it around molded areas.*

Drawing the entire panel design on the panel board may be helpful. At least mark the positions of any seams, pattern, or material changes or other guidelines that will help align it properly. Lay the covering over panel board and line it up correctly. Mark and cut it, leaving 1-1/2 to 2in on all sides for attachment.

If the panel is to be covered with a single piece of fabric, spread it face down on your work table and lay the panel board on it. Trace the perimeter of the board onto the fabric and draw a second outline two inches from the edge. Cut on the second outline to allow material to fold over and attach to the board.

If the fabric has a woven pattern or pressed-in design such as pleats or squares, lay it face up on top of the panel board to position the design correctly. Also, check that the material lies in the right direction. For example, you want the nap of velour to lie down like the flow of a waterfall.

Installing the Panel Cover

When correctly positioned, fold back half of the cover, apply adhesive to both surfaces, and careful-ly smooth the cover into place. Fold back the other half and follow the same gluing procedure. Trim to two inches from the edge of the panel board.

Turn the panel over so the cover is face down, and apply adhesive to the edges of the fabric and the panel board. When the cement is tacky, pull the fabric over the edge of the board and press it down. Start in the center of each side and work out to the corners, pulling the material tight. Turn the panel over periodically to check that everything is still lined up correctly.

Modern adhesives are quite good, but stapling around the edge will insure against the cover creeping and going slack in time. Staples must be long enough to hold the fabric and any padding securely, yet not penetrate through the board. Staple the middle first and work toward each edge at 1/2in intervals.

If the material or padding is bulky, trim some away at the corners or make pie-shaped cuts so it will fold over neatly with only one or two layers to staple through. To finish off, trim the excess material 1/4in inside the staple line.

A dull butter knife or rounded off putty knife (shown) helps work the material into corners. After you form the material, trim away excess material, leaving just enough to fold over the edge and glue.

Door and Side Panel Recovery

Door and side panels began to take on a third dimension during the fifties. Interior designers started integrating the hardware into the panel, sculpturing it around the armrest, and creating handles and window controls to blend with the panel design. In some cases, vinyl is molded and bonded directly to the panel. Sometimes separate panels of plastic, fiberglass, fiberboard, metal, or wood attach to the main panel.

Some elements of these molded trim panels are impossible to duplicate exactly. The example shown, from a 1965 Thunderbird, has a fluted feature molded to the top of the panel. Fortunately, on this example, that feature was still in good shape. If it hadn't been, the owner would have had the choice of trying to find a good used one (new reproductions are not available) and dyeing it the desired color or creating a similar effect by forming vinyl over dense foam and sewing or stapling it into sharp rolls.

Vinyl upholstery is really quite durable. Where it hasn't been subjected to a lot of wear, it often doesn't require replacement. The door and quarter panels of my 1965 Chrysler 300 still look fine after nearly thirty years of service.

After cleaning it well, examine the piece you're restoring to determine how much of it is still serviceable. Also, consider whether the resources— correct material, replacement panels, etc.—are available to restore it correctly. The vinyl covering and some of the molded foam padding on the T-bird door panels mentioned above had broken up from years of use, but the fluted formations and the rest of the panels were still good. Upholsterer Randy Vajgrt determined covering the middle portion of the panels with new vinyl and cleaning and conditioning the rest would put them back in good condition. Although the original covering was molded in one piece, stainless steel trim would hide the seams where new material was added.

Since the vinyl cover is bonded to the backing in this case, trying to remove it would damage the foam, so new material is applied over the old. Thoroughly clean the surface to be covered with lacquer thinner or wax and grease remover so glue will stick. Cover and smooth the damaged area with wide masking tape. If chunks of foam are missing, trim back to a smooth, even surface, then

In this case, Randy Vajgrt had to drill and pop rivet the top door edge trim back on.

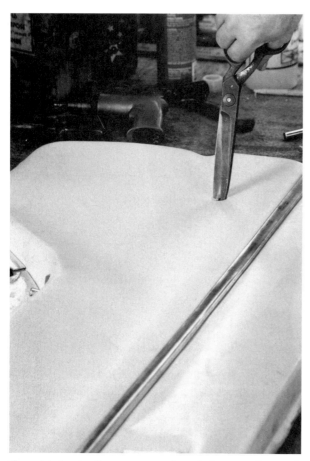

To cut holes in the new cover for window cranks, push slightly opened scissors into the hole and snip a slit. Turn the scissors ninety degrees and repeat. Do the same to cut out the hand grip hole, and glue the ends into the hole.

cut and glue in pieces of foam to fill out the area to its original contours.

Cut a piece of matching vinyl to fit the area to be covered with a few inches to spare on all sides. Since it would be hard to stretch the vinyl around a tight curve on the back corner of the armrest, Randy slit and sewed it for a snug fit. Not quite like the factory, but neat enough that it looks like it could be. Mask off the portions of the panel not being covered. Coat both the back of the vinyl and the panel with contact cement. When the cement becomes tacky, lay the vinyl in place and press down the flat areas. An extra pair of hands may be needed here, or you may want to glue only half of the panel at a time.

A heat gun or hair dryer warms the vinyl and makes it more pliable to stretch and fit the contours of the panel. A tool such as a rounded putty knife or a dull butter knife helps tuck the vinyl into sharp corners. Trim the vinyl to shape, and cut holes where necessary for handles and other hardware. Reinstall the stainless trim, clean off any extra glue, and the panel is ready to go back into the car.

Panel Installation

Locate holes for the handles, armrest attachment screws and any other door trim. Make cross cuts for the larger holes. Pierce the cover with an awl to make holes for trim tabs. Reinstall any trim and hardware that attaches to the door or side panel and install the spring clips. Position the panel and feel behind to guide each spring clip into the correct hole. Seat the clips with a firm push or a sharp blow with the heel of your hand.

Install armrests, handles, and other hardware that mount to the door.

Quarter Panels

Recovering and installing rear door panels on four-door cars and rear quarter panels on two-door cars generally follow the above procedures. Be sure to line up any character lines with those on the door panels. Some hardtops have fixed armrest panels and convertibles have top well panels that must be covered while in the car. The procedure is the same, just a little harder to accomplish.

Strip the old upholstery and padding, noting the materials used and how they're attached. Cut and fit foam padding and glue it to the panel with enough to roll over the edge. Make up the upholstery covering, fit and glue it to the padded panels.

Windlace Installation

Take note of the attachment method when you remove the old windlace. It may involve one or a combination of tacks, staples, clips, screws, or molding. Over sedan doors, it usually attaches underneath the edge of the headliner; there may also be wire-on welting to cover the headliner tacking. In some places—like in front of the doors—the binding may slide into a channel in the body metal.

Replacement windlacing is available from many restoration supply sources, as well as general upholstery suppliers. It's possible neither will have an exact match for some unusual models, but if you send a sample, they should be able to come close or at least offer something to closely coordinate with your upholstery.

You may need to install new tacking strips from an antique upholstery supplier. If there's no provision for attaching them with screws or pop rivets, you can glue them in with a strong adhesive like Liquid Nails and clamp them with Vise Grips until it's set.

Hold the strip of windlace in place and mark where there are sharp bends around corners. Make crosscuts or pie-shaped cuts at 1/2in intervals to prevent bunching in these spots. Cut the windlace to length plus a little extra to tuck under door sills or carpeting.

You may have to loosen the ends of the dashboard and windshield molding to install the front windlace. Also, remove the door sill plates if you

The only deviation from original is a seam Randy had to sew into a tight back corner where it was impossible to get the new vinyl to conform.

Upholstery may have originally been tacked to the wooden framework of an early car, but if you'd rather use spring clips, one way is to screw flat washers to the wood to receive the clips.

haven't already. Trial-fit the windlace, allowing an extra inch or two at each end, and trim. It may help to hold the windlace in place with contact cement while determining the placement.

Start with the bottom where the end tucks under the door sill plate. Work around the opening, pulling the lacing taut as you go, and stay-tack at two- or three-inch intervals. Work the selvage between the door pillar and the dash in front. When the windlace is adjusted correctly along the full length, secure it with staples, tacks or other original attachment method. To finish off the ends, open the selvage and cut off the core even with the panel edge. Fold the cover material over the end and bury the tail behind the windlace.

Reinstall the handles, hardware and trim, and the panel is complete.

Chapter Nine

Headliner

The ceiling of your car, known as the headliner, presents some unique problems when restoring the interior. On one hand, it may very well be in the best shape of any component. Located "above the action," so to speak, it is out of direct sunlight and moisture and relatively free from wear. The original, twenty-year-old vinyl headliner in a Pontiac I owned cleaned up fine and did not have to be replaced, even though the car had been parked in a field for some time.

Yet, headliners are subject to a variety of hazards, some of which don't affect other parts of the interior. In early cars, the headliner was tacked to wooden bows. Until the mid-thirties, when the industry introduced all-steel tops, cars had fabric inserts in the top. These often developed leaks in time, and moisture stained the headliner. On steel-top cars from the thirties through the sixties headliners are hung from steel bows that slip through sheaths called listing strips and attach to the side rails of the top. Whatever wrapping or treatment was done to keep bows from rusting did-

Consider yourself lucky if your 40-year-old restoration candidate is better than this. The headliner is completely gone, but some of the insulation remains. Headliner bows are in place and can be reused.

n't always last, so rust can stain the headliner. Sometimes the thread rots and gives way, even though the material is still good.

Rodents seem to love to chew up headliners, I don't know if for food or to line their nests. They stand on the sun visors to get at the headliner, so turning the visors down when storing the car can help prevent this damage. Moths love headliners, too, which is why car collectors often put mothballs inside when the car is stored.

Manufacturers began in the sixties to cement the headliner fabric to a rigid shell molded to fit the inside of the top, and this type of installation became pretty universal by the end of the seventies. The problem with these headliners is that the foam padding between the fabric and the shell deteriorates, and the headliner falls down.

In this chapter we'll take a look at the three types of headliner installations, how to remove and replace them, and how to make a new headliner.

If your headliner isn't stained and is free of holes or tears, you may get by with just a good

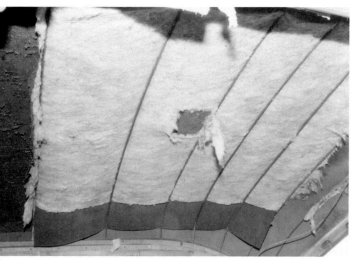

With the headliner fabric gone, construction of insulation padding and bows in this 1952 Ford Victoria is evident.

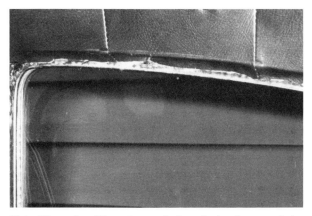

This Chevy headliner is stapled and glued around the rear quarter window opening. Removing window moldings will reveal the installation method.

The 1965 Ford headliner is folded over and glued to the edge of the roof channel. The nylon strip grips the edge, and a stainless steel garnish molding covers it all.

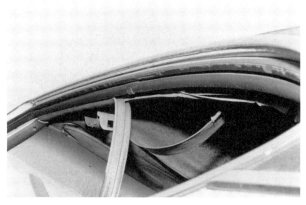

The headliner in this Olds Cutlass, as well as Cougars and others, glues over the lip inside the roof, and the edge is covered with a flexible plastic molding.

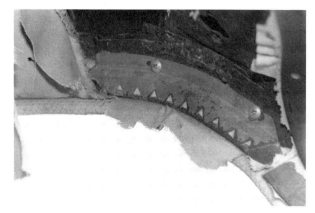

It's impossible to remove a headliner intact from the grip of teeth like this. Hanging a new headliner with this system, used by GM in the fifties, is also a trick.

On a 1964 Dart the headliner pulls over the edge and is held by teeth and glue. A metal garnish molding covers the raw edge.

Headliner bows on this 1951 Ford snap into sockets along the edge. Twist them forward or back to remove or install them. Number the bows to keep them in order, and note whether they were in the top or bottom holes. Bows mount with bolts in some cars.

Number the panels on the old headliner from front to rear before taking it apart to use the panels for patterns. Also mark the center line, side to side. Transfer these marks to the new panels. Use a soft lead pencil or chalk. Marker or ball point pen can bleed through to the outside.

cleaning. Use a soft brush and a vacuum cleaner to get dust and dirt out of cloth. Vinyl can be scrubbed with a cloth wrung out of soapy water, or with a commercial upholstery cleaner. Don't get the headliner too wet. You may want to take it out to give it a more thorough cleaning. A few of the more expensive early cars actually had leather headliners, which—of course—would require special attention. See the earlier discussion on cleaning and restoring leather.

Headliners Hung from Bows

From the mid-thirties, when solid steel tops became standard, to the late sixties, when molded headliners replaced them, headliners were suspended from rods or bows. The edges were secured to the body and covered by moldings or windlace. Since cars from this era are being restored more commonly today than older models with wooden bows, we'll use them to detail the procedure and discuss a little later the procedural differences for earlier models.

Removal

To remove the headliner, first remove sun visors, window moldings, and any hardware or trim that prevents free access to the headliner. Replace the screws in their respective holes; this will not only keep track of them, but help you locate these attachment points when they're covered by the new headliner.

Note how the fabric attaches around the edges. On many cars it is tacked or stapled to a fiberboard tack strip. On others, it is inserted into retaining strips with teeth that grip the fabric, or glued over a lip inside the edge of the roof with a channel strip to hold it in place. With speed of assembly essential, on later cars the headliner is merely glued in. Carefully take the old headliner loose from the edges. A deep notch filed or ground into the blade of an old screwdriver makes a fine tack removal tool.

The bows either snap into sockets or attach with screws to the steel framework on the edges of the top. Take them loose one at a time—snap-in bows usually must be rotated toward the rear for removal—and slide them out of the sheathes, or listing strips. Mark each bow with a number or a set of dots to indicate its position from front to rear; they must be reinstalled in the same order. If they show any signs of rust, remove the rust with sandpaper, steel wool, or a Scotch Brite pad, and refinish them with rust-inhibiting paint.

To use the headliner as a pattern to make a replacement, number the panels from front to rear. Then separate them at the seams and stack them in order.

Remove all old tacks and staples from the tack strips, if that's what your car has. Replace the strips if they're in poor condition. Now is the time

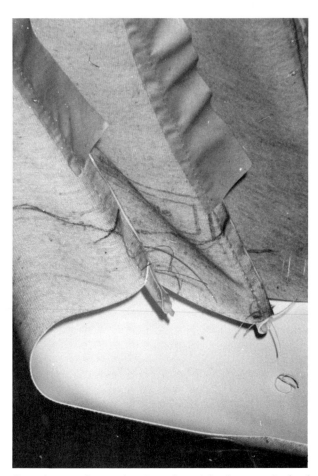

Sew the panels together in order with about an inch of seam. If the headliner had welting between panels, sew it to one panel first, then attach the second panel. Sew the listing strips to the seams after panels are sewn together.

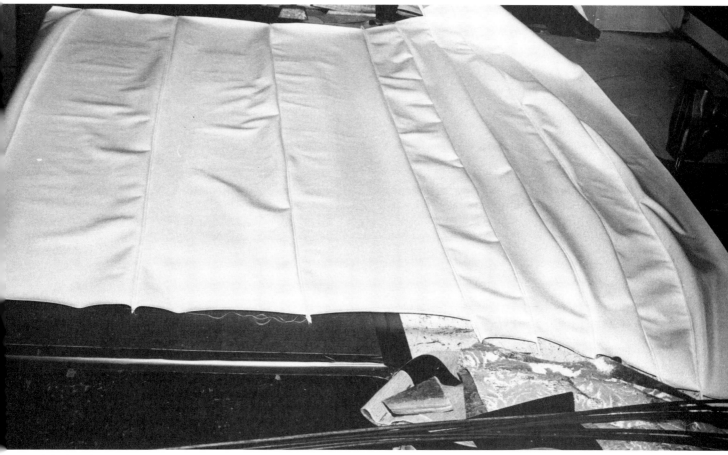

The headliner is all sewn together and ready to hang. The edges will be trimmed after installation.

to take care of any other things the headliner hides, such as replacing dome light wires and refinishing attachment strips and window moldings. Replace insulation that may be cemented to the roof; if your car didn't come with it, you might want to add some. It will be out of sight and can help protect the interior from extreme temperatures and noise. There are some good glue-in products such as Kool Kar on the market.

Constructing a Headliner

Ready-made headliners can save a lot of work, but they may not be available for all models. Some suppliers sell universal headliners designed to adapt to several different models, so compare it with the old one to be sure it's going to fit properly. If you need or want to make your own, it's not a daunting task. Just measure carefully and sew straight seams.

If you followed the removal instructions, you have a stack of numbered fabric panels to use as patterns. In the event your car's headliner is completely missing, make patterns by measuring the length of the bows and the distance between the bows for the dimensions of each panel. Though it takes some additional time, it would be advisable to make up a headliner out of some cheap material and try it for fit, then take it apart and use it for patterns.

Lay out the headliner material face down on a clean work table. Take care to keep your hands clean at all times while working on the headliner. Lay your pattern pieces on the new fabric and trace around them. Work on two or three panels at a time, arranging them to make best use of the material. Mark lines for the seams, and leave an inch of sewing allowance for each seam when you cut out the panels. Number them like the old ones, and stack them in order.

Lay the number two panel face to face with number one, align the marked seam lines or the edges and pin them. Sew the two panels together along the marked seam. Then proceed to sew panel three to panel two and so forth from front to rear. Although it was mainly a custom touch, some headliners might have had piping at the seams. If that is the case, sew the piping to one panel first, then sew the second panel to the first with another seam.

Sew the listing strips to the sewing allowance of each seam after the entire headliner is sewn together. Pre-made cotton listing strips are available from auto upholstery suppliers, or you can make them from strips of flexible fabric two inches wide. Fold the strip in half lengthwise, press the fold with a steam iron, and sew the open edge to the headliner seam. The strip forms an envelope that the bow slips through. Positioning strips on the side of the seam toward the rear of the car makes the headliner hang better. The listing strips don't need to go all the way to the edge of the headliner, and they may need to be cut back during installation to allow the liner to pull snug without wrinkling.

Installation

Insert the support bows by the numbers into the listing strips and center them. Trim the listings back about two inches from the bow ends. Fold the headliner and bows like a convertible top, and begin the installation at the rear bow. Along

Insert bows into the listing strips in proper order. If they show signs of rust, clean and paint them so they won't stain the new headliner. To install the bows, place the ends in the sockets and pivot the bow from rear to front until it's seated vertically and snug to the roof. Center the headliner and pull out the wrinkles side to side and front to rear.

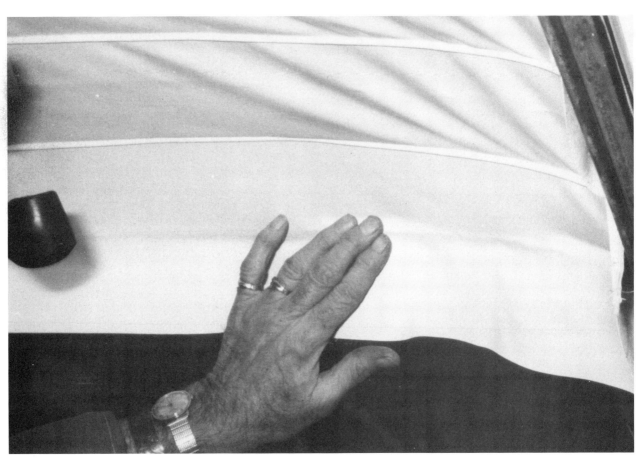

Apply trim adhesive to the rear attachment strip. Then pull the headliner taut, press it against the strip and pull it away. A little glue will mark the contact line. Apply cement to the headliner along that line. When the ce- *ment is tacky, stretch and press the headliner into place, working from the center out to the edges. Pull out wrinkles. The material will slacken with time, so it must be taut to begin with.*

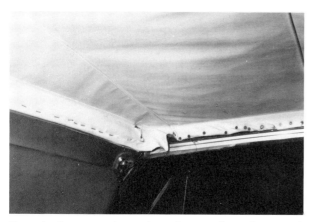

Stretch the seams into place first and staple or tack them on both edges (heating vinyl carefully with a heat gun or hair dryer will make it easier to work into position). Then staple the sides solidly, working from the middle toward the front and rear and alternating from side to side. Once secured, trim the edges and reinstall the trim moldings.

with the sockets or screw attachment at the ends, one or more bows may be secured in the middle by prongs or clips. Install the other bows, working from back to front. Pull the fabric snug front to rear and side to side, working out all the wrinkles and making sure it fits properly.

Beginning at the rear again, apply contact cement to the tack strip, pull the headliner fabric over the strip and press it down briefly, then remove. A line of cement will be left on the fabric to mark where it attaches. Apply more cement to that area, and let both surfaces dry until the adhesive is tacky. Pull the headliner into place in the middle, then work out in each direction, pulling the fabric taut to the rear and side as you go. When the back has dried so it's not likely to pull loose, go to the front and follow the same procedure.

After ascertaining that the liner is straight, return to the back and staple or tack at half-inch intervals from the center out a few inches at a time. Alternate from back to front to help keep the fabric

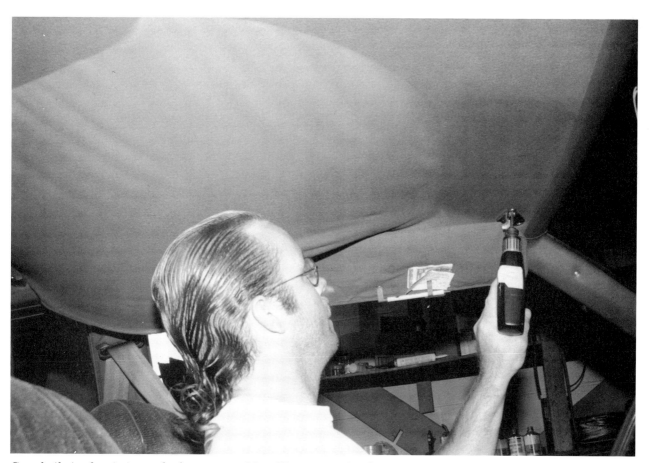

Cars built in the sixties and after cemented headliner fabric to a rigid, molded shell. The problem with these headliners is that the foam padding between the fabric and the shell deteriorates, and the headliner falls down (as shown). The first step to the repair is to remove all trim, dome light and moldings that hold or cover the headliner shell.

Remove the shell from the car. Some cars have reusable clips on the windshield molding while others have to be cut and replaced. When the shell is loose, maneuver it out of the car, usually by the right door. Pull the cover

off and scrape the remaining foam off the shell with a wire brush or your hands. Blow off all loose particles. Repair any cracks or broken spots with masking tape.

smooth and tight until both back and front are secured all the way across.

The sides are next. On a sedan, the windlacing probably attaches underneath the headliner; if so, be sure to install it first. Detail on windlace installation is included with sidewall reupholstering in Chapter Eight. Start at the mid-point, specifically the middle seam, making sure it forms a straight line across the car's roof. Pull taut and staple or stay-tack the seam to the trim strip. Then attach the seams just forward and back of the middle seam the same way. Go to the other side of the car and repeat the procedure. Alternate sides and work from the center toward both ends until all the seams are secured and the wrinkles worked out. When everything looks good, go back and tack or staple between the seams at half-inch intervals.

This type of installation may use wire-on welting to cover the tacks. Place it snug against the windlace, tack or staple it in place, then fold the wire-on over itself to hide the tacks, and press down smooth. You may want to tap it with a body hammer to make it lie down smooth and flat.

Instead of tacks or staples, the headliner fabric in some cars tucks into a slot in a retainer strip along the edge, where teeth hold it in place. A putty knife or kitchen knife with the blade rounded off so it won't poke holes in the fabric is the best tool for working the fabric into the slot. As you do with staples or tacks, pull it taut as you go, work back and forth and do a few inches at a time.

If the headliner edges are glued, follow the same procedure you did for gluing the fabric at the back and front. Apply cement to both surfaces and let it set up. Start at the middle of each side, pull the headliner taut and glue it over the lip of the top frame. Work toward the front and the rear and from side to side, pulling the material snug as you go. Secure the edge with whatever type of trim was used originally.

Early Car Headliner Removal

Installation details varied widely on early cars, so take note of how your headliner and the components around it are assembled. Early cars often have upholstered panels covering the edges of the headliner around the side and rear windows, possibly even above the windshield. Removing the window garnish moldings should reveal how these panels are attached, probably with some combination of tacks, cement, and screws. Some installations used wire-on welting to cover the tacks. After being tacked on, the wire-on is folded over itself and pressed down to form a smooth, finished edge. Of course, you must remove the dome light, sun visors, windlacing, and anything else that's in the way of the headliner.

After loosening the edges of the headliner, you'll see how it hangs from listing strips tacked to the front edge of the wooden top bows. The procedure for making a tacked-in headliner is the same as for bow-hung liners outlined in the preceding section. If you obtained a ready-made headliner from one of the suppliers listed in the Appendix, you can proceed to install it.

Installation on Wooden Bows

Like bow-hung headliners, those that attach to wooden bows are made with listing strips sewn into

the seams. Instead of a rod or bow inserted through a sheath, however, the listing strips tack or staple to the front face of the wooden bows. First, measure and mark the exact center of the bows and the center of the liner or listing strips. Starting with the rear-most bow, tack in the center, then work out to each side, pulling the fabric taut as you go. Stay-tacking at one- to two-inch intervals will hold the liner in position, but is easy to take loose and redo if necessary. When everything looks straight and true, go back and tack or staple at 1/2in intervals.

Move forward to the next bow and so on until the headliner is attached to all the bows. The edges of the liner were probably originally tacked to a wooden framework or tack strip. You can replace it the same way, but stapling with a staple gun may be easier. Gluing it will also make the connection more secure. Follow the procedure outlined previously for gluing and tacking the headliner edges on a bow-hung installation.

The upper panels on the sides and back are recovered with the appropriate material as you would side walls or other rigid panels. If new panels are

Lay the new headliner material over the shell and cut it roughly to size. Fold back half of the cover and apply adhesive to both the cover and the shell. When cement is tacky, pull the cover over the shell and smooth it into place, working from the middle out. When the adhesive sets, trim the edges. Some can be trimmed to the edge of the shell while a little extra must be left on others. Note this when you take the old one out.

Cut out holes for the dome light and any trim. Reinstall the headliner shell by reversing the steps followed to remove it. Adjust and center it before tightening moldings.

needed, cut them from panel board. To make panels curve around the rear quarters, cut panel board to the correct size and shape, then moisten it and bend it to the necessary shape. You can either tie a cord around the panel to hold the curve or tack the panel into the car until it dries and sets.

After covering, reinstall these panels following the original methods. As mentioned, they may have been tacked to the wooden framework, covering the edges of the headliner, and the tack line covered with wire-on welting. Some installations that didn't use welting are a bit trickier. You must tack through the upholstery cloth, then use a needle to carefully work the fabric out to cover the tack heads. The fabric nap should hide the holes.

Finishing Up

All headlining materials tend to stretch, which can make them sag and wrinkle a few days or weeks after installation. It's imperative to stretch the liner taut as you put it in so it won't sag noticeably when it begins to relax. Alternating from side to side and stay-tacking or stapling the lining in place first is important. Going back to do the finish stapling gives you a second chance to pull it tight, even if it means replacing the original staples after taking out the slack.

In spite of your best effort, some wrinkles and slack may remain. Even experienced trimmers don't always get them all out. That's why they keep a steamer around. Applying steam to a woven fabric headliner and steam or heat to vinyl can shrink it enough to remove the wrinkles.

The ideal apparatus is an electric steamer with a hose or wand that can reach into confined areas. If possible, apply the steam to the back side of the lining by inserting the wand or hose through the dome light hole or an opening around the edge. Otherwise apply it to the outside with the regular steamer outlet. Don't soak the fabric, just dampen it. It should stretch as it dries. Repeat the process if wrinkles remain.

If no steamer is available, dampen woven fabric a small area at a time with water from a spray bottle, then heat and dry it with an electric hair dryer. The hair dryer works without water to both shrink vinyl and make it pliable, but be very careful not to get it too close or hold it too long in one place.

To prevent twisting the material when you reinstall screws, locate the holes and make a hole in the fabric first.

When the headliner is hung and tacked in place, trim it with scissors or a blade so trim and moldings will hide the edges. Locate the screws that were inserted to mark the positions of the dome light, sun visors, and other hardware. With a razor blade, make a small slit over each screw, remove the screws, and reinstall the hardware. Finally, reinstall the window and side moldings to complete the job.

Recovering a Molded Headliner

In the late sixties manufacturers began installing a shell molded to conform to the inside of the top. The shell is fiberboard, fiberglass, Styrofoam, or a combination of these. On some models—especially station wagons and cheaper lines—the fiberboard material was painted to coordinate with the interior. Most installations, however, are finished with a vinyl or cloth headliner backed by a thin layer of foam, which glues directly to the shell—until it falls down.

The problem can be either with the adhesive or the foam. Either can deteriorate with heat, age, and moisture and separate, letting the headliner droop onto the passengers' heads. In temperate ar-

eas a headliner can be expected to stay in place for ten years or more, but in hot, arid areas it may not last more than five years.

Attempting to simply re-glue the headliner isn't likely to be successful; you'll only be gluing fabric to already deteriorating foam. Some upholsterers sew either the old or new fabric to the shell or install buttons to hold it up, but that destroys the authenticity.

The only sure cure is to install new foam-backed headliner material. It's not very difficult or expensive. Suppliers have universal or specific replacement material cut to fit most popular models. Unless the car has been through an unusual disaster such as a flood or fire, the ceiling shell should be reusable, but be careful taking it down.

First, remove all the hardware—visors, dome light, coat hooks—and put the fasteners in a safe place. Remove the moldings above the windshield and side windows. Some are held by screws, some by reusable clips and some by clips that have to be cut or broken and replaced with new ones when the trim goes back in. Attachment methods vary from car to car and from year to year. Figure out

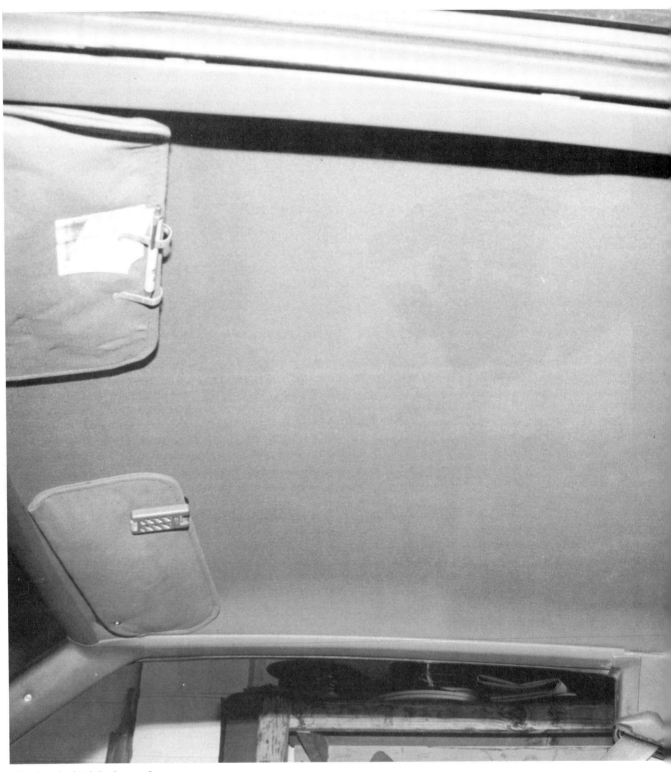

The finished job looks good as new.

how your headliner was put in as you disassemble it, then reverse the procedure to reinstall it.

Now you can see how the headliner shell is held in. You may have to remove more moldings or clips to get it loose, but in many cases just loosening the rear moldings will allow the shell to slide forward and out. Maneuver it down below the steering wheel and rotate it ninety degrees to take it out the right

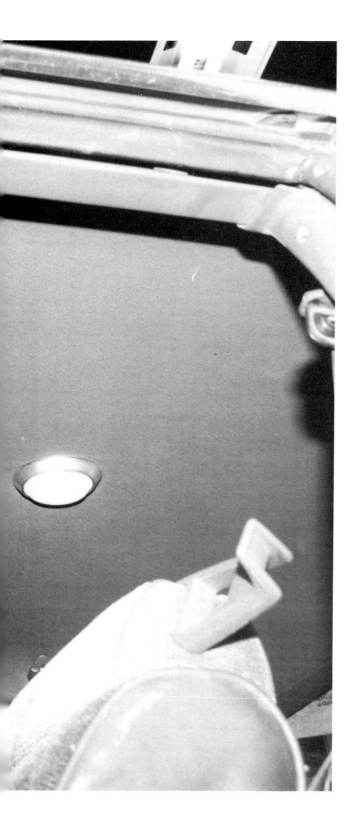

Lay the headliner shell on a flat surface and pull the fabric off. A wire brush works well to remove all the old foam down to a clean surface glue can adhere to. A wire brush attachment on an electric drill will work, but be careful not to damage the shell material. Also, some shells are fiberglass like home insulation, which a wire brush will ruin. Rub the foam off with your hands on this type. Blow the surface clean with compressed air.

Check the shell for damage. If there are cracks or broken pieces, repair them with masking tape.

Lay the new foam-backed headliner material over the shell and cut it to size, leaving several inches on each side. Fold half of the liner back, apply contact cement to both the shell and the foam backing of the headliner and allow it to dry to the tacky stage. Heat and humidity will determine how quickly that occurs.

Several types of trim adhesive are available from upholstery or restoration suppliers. Commercial shops buy Weldwood Contact Adhesive, 3M All-Purpose Trim Adhesive, or similar products in bulk and apply them with a pressure pot or a spray gun. A home compressor and spray equipment may work for you, although it may be necessary to thin the cement. Otherwise, aerosol cans of adhesive are available, or it can be obtained in cans or tubes for brushing on.

Contact cement applied to both surfaces sticks when the surfaces are pressed together. It's somewhat forgiving, meaning you can pull the material loose and reposition it within a five- to ten-minute period.

When the cement is tacky, fold the coated half of the headliner material into place on the shell and press it down with your hands. Work from the center out to the edges. Don't stretch the material, but tuck it into the corners. Then fold back the other half and do the same thing.

When you take the old headliner down notice how much of the material extends beyond the edge of the shell. In some cases it is trimmed even with the edge, in others there will be a half inch or so to spare because the shell is a close fit to the trim moldings, and the extra material fills any gaps. Trim the edges of your new headliner accordingly.

Locate and cut out the holes for the dome light, visors and other hardware. Note which holes are used when you take the liner out. If the same shell is used in several models, it may have holes your car doesn't need.

Maneuver the headliner back into the car and slide it into position on the sides and back. Center it and make any adjustments before tightening the rear window molding. Install the sun visors to position the headliner at the front. Use an awl to locate the screw holes and pierce the fabric so the screws won't twist and pull it as they go in. Reinstall the rest of the moldings and interior hardware.

door. Be careful not to force or damage the shell taking it out. There are no replacements for many models, so if it's damaged beyond repair, you'll be out scrounging salvage yards for a replacement.

Chapter Ten

Carpeting

There was a time when you could tell the price class of a car by looking at the floor. The cheap models had rubber mats. Move up the line a bit and you got scratchy, but durable, horsehair carpeting. At the top end you might get the feeling of being in a drawing room with luxurious wool carpeting covering the floor. Combinations were sometimes installed, such as mats in front and carpet in the rear. Rubber mats sometimes had carpet inserts, but later, as carpeting became more universal, the reverse was true—full carpeting with rubber (or vinyl) inserts in high-wear areas.

Today, most new cars—and trucks, too—come fully carpeted. For many years carpet material has also been used on sidewall panels, kick panels, and seat bolsters for both decoration and protection.

In case you're restoring an economy model that came with rubber mats, if strict authenticity isn't a high priority, you may want to consider laying down carpet to give it a bit more style and comfort. In fact, it could be more practical. Authentic carpeting may be easier to come by than original-style floor mats.

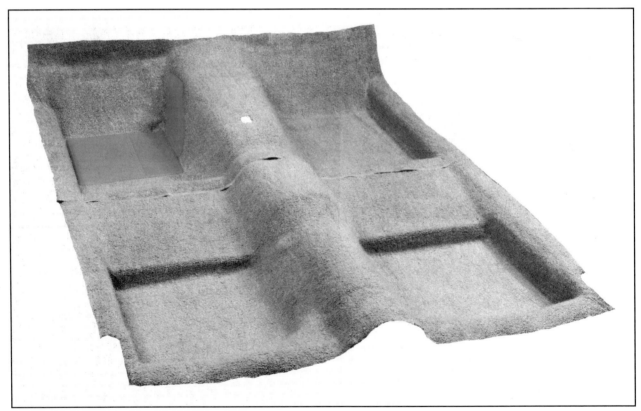

Ready-to-install carpet cut and molded to fit is available for most models from firms like Auto Custom Carpet. If your vehicle's floor is quite irregular, with sunken foot wells like the one shown, molded carpet assures a neat fit with minimal work.

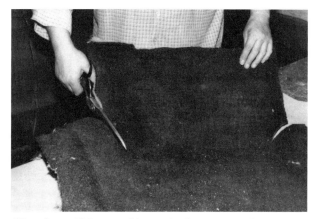

Worn but still intact, this original carpet can be removed and used as a pattern for making new carpet. If a molded carpet is being used as a pattern, cut the corners where the foot wells sink in to make it lie flat.

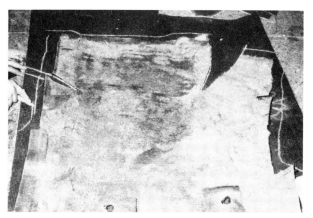

Lay the old carpet, back side up, on the back side of the new carpet and trace around it. Leave one to two inches extra around the border, or draw a second line at that distance. Mark the spots where you cut the old carpet and the location of holes for pedals, shift levers and seat belts.

Carpeting gives a car a finished look and cushioning underfoot, besides helping muffle noise and insulate the interior against heat and cold.

Carpet Characteristics

Carpet made for automotive applications has specific characteristics, since it must withstand temperature extremes, certain wear patterns and moisture. Although it may be similar in composition, most household carpeting is unsuitable for a vehicle.

The pile of your car's original carpeting is easy to determine. The pile, or nap, consists of threads or yarn woven in loops and bonded to a backing. Left this way it is known as loop pile. The pile may be low or nearly flat, or the loops may be longer for a deeper pile. Sometimes the loops are formed into rows or a square pattern, but more often they are random.

The other type of pile is cut pile, where the ends of the loops are shaved off and the fibers stick up like brush bristles. Again, the pile may be short or deep. The usual depth of cut pile is 3/8in, of plush or deep pile, 5/8in.

A tighter weave increases firmness and durability in both loop pile and cut pile. Most suppliers are glad to furnish samples to compare with the original carpeting in your car.

While pile is easy to identify, the original fiber is more difficult. And it may not make a lot of difference, anyhow, because you may be stuck with whatever is available. Correct replacement carpeting isn't made for all cars, only the more popular ones. Some suppliers don't specify what the fiber is, so you can assume it's a synthetic made to appear as original. Nylon, for example, can be made to duplicate many different materials. If your model is supposed to have wool, you may end up with nylon that only an expert can tell from wool.

Wilton wool, with a short pile, and longer-piled Hargarn wool were the most common auto floor coverings in the pre-synthetic days of the thirties and forties. An 80/20 rayon/nylon blend with a heavy, twisted loop pile became common in the fifties and sixties, along with some 100% nylon loop. Some models of that era came with a special 80/20 loop pile containing black flecks and known as Tuxedo Pile or "salt-and-pepper." Daytona Loop, with a low, tightly woven looped-face appearance, was original on some fifties models.

Nylon loop was the most common style of the sixties, giving way to nylon cut pile almost exclusively in the seventies and eighties. In later years higher-priced cars have been fitted with plush pile.

Replacement carpeting may be of the original fibers or others, including 80/20 nylon/rayon blend, acrylic or polyester.

Purchased in bulk, carpeting usually has a rubberized backing. Unbacked carpet material is also available and should be specified for sewing with other materials to upholster side panels. Ready-made carpeting for specific models usually has jute, foam, or fiber padding attached, also. When cutting and sewing your own, you'll probably want to use original-type padding, but since it isn't seen, you might consider a different type or thicker padding for insulation and noise reduction.

Molded Versus Sewn

There are three carpet replacement options. Whether all three are open to you depends upon the availability of ready-made replacement carpet for your project. First, carpeting is available by the yard for you to cut, sew and finish yourself. Second, there are replacements sewn to fit the floor contours of specific models. Third is carpet molded to fit the floor contours.

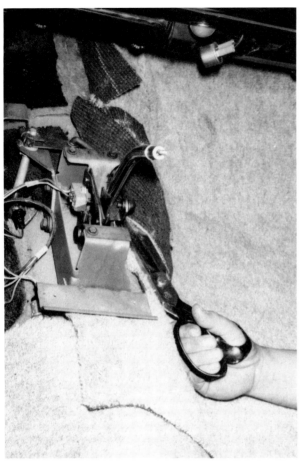

Install the padding and trial-fit the carpet. Trim around the gear shift and pedals as required.

Contour-sewn carpet was original equipment in most models from the twenties to the sixties. Some suppliers offer contour-sewn sets for later models, also. Ready to install, it is seamed, primarily under the dash, to fit the floor pan contour and finished with the correct binding, grommets and heel pads.

Since floors of modern cars have gained more curves and dips with foot wells and higher driveshaft tunnels, carpets to cover them are press-molded to the floor pan contour, eliminating the seams. Replacements are made the same way, with necessary heel pads and grommets installed. Many are one-piece, others have separate front and back sections.

Attachment Methods

Carpeting in early cars was held in place with fasteners and could be removed easily for drying and cleaning. Around 1940 manufacturers started gluing carpet to the padding, which was, in turn, cemented to the floor. The next advance was to eliminate border bindings and hide the carpet edges under door sill plates. Carpet is secured this way on most cars since 1955.

Check with suppliers listed in the Appendix for contour-sewn or molded replacement carpets, or for bulk carpeting to make your own.

Making a Pattern

Assuming you have decided to make your own carpet from scratch, you'll first need a pattern. Keep the original carpet as intact as possible as you remove it, and it can serve as a pattern. Otherwise, clear the floor area and lay down heavy paper, pushing it tight into corners and tracing the outline with a pencil or felt marker. Include the locations of pedals, shift levers and other components for which cutouts are required. Make separate patterns for each individual piece of carpet, for example, one piece for the front floor and another for the rear.

Add an inch or more in each direction if the carpet is to go under sill plates. It can be trimmed after fitting. For carpet with bound edges, allow an extra 1/2in for sewing the binding on.

You may find gluing the paper pattern to a sheet of cardboard makes it easier to work with. Lay the pattern on the carpet and trace around it with chalk. Use a utility knife or upholstery shears to cut out the carpet.

Carpet Padding

Since the thickness of the padding will affect how the carpet fits, install it first. Jute felt, or simply jute, is the usual material. It's available in bulk from suppliers of antique car carpet or upholstery materials. One of them, the Auto-Mat Co., claims padding adds forty percent to the life of the carpet.

Follow your pattern, as well as the original installation, to cut the padding to size and shape. Sometimes the original padding didn't cover the entire floor, but use your own judgment. Since it will be out of sight, appearance is not so important. You can cut and piece it into irregular areas. Trim the edges about an inch short of the carpet edge; the padding doesn't have to tuck under door sill plates or upholstered panels.

Be sure the floor is thoroughly cleaned and, if necessary, refinished with rust-inhibiting paint. After fitting a piece of padding to the floor, fold back half at a time, apply adhesive to both surfaces, and press the padding into place.

Fitting the Carpet

After marking the carpet from your pattern and cutting it to shape, trial-fit it in the car and check to see that marks for cutting seams, pedal holes, etc. are correct. If pedals or gear shift knobs are removable, you need only make a hole for the shaft. Otherwise, make a single cut from the top edge of the carpet to the pedal location, then enlarge the hole around the pedal. The carpet will lie

Sew the V-shaped cuts together by folding the sides of the cut together, face to face, and stitching about 1/4in *from the edge. This will pull the corners together to make the carpet fit the floor shape.*

flat, the nap hiding the cut. Finish the hole with binding or a grommet as per the original. Trial-fit again after making the cuts.

Construction of the old carpet may dictate how the new fits the front floor and transmission tunnel. The main body of the carpet usually fits the floor, sloping toe boards and straight portion of the driveshaft tunnel. V-shaped cuts are required to make the carpet fit over the transmission hump under the dashboard. Finish the cuts with binding if that's how it was done originally. Otherwise, the cuts can be sewn together by hand on the back side; when it's glued down the nap will hide the seam.

Another way to join two pieces of carpet is to sew a strip of vinyl or tightly woven fabric under the edge of one piece, then butt the other piece up against the first and sew it to the strip. The pile will cover the seam. When sewing through carpet, open a channel in the pile with your fingers; the seam will lie down in the channel and be invisible.

It may be possible to salvage the heel pads or other inserts from your original carpet, or reproductions may be available. Locating the pads, then shaving down the nap and cementing them in place provides a neat, secure installation.

Binding

Carpet binding isn't required on later models where the edges are secured under door sill plates and upholstered panels. For earlier models, the usual binding material is vinyl in a matching or contrasting color. Cut strips two to three inches wide and long enough to cover the edge being bound. Refer to chapter six for techniques for piecing together longer strips.

Place the binding face down on the carpet with the edges aligned. If the pile is heavy, shave it along the edge to make sewing easier. Sew the binding to the carpet 1/4–1/2in from the edge. Then sew a second, reinforcing seam next to the first. Fold the binding over, right side out, and pull it snugly around the carpet edge. On the face of the carpet, sew just outside the folded edge of the binding strip to attach the binding to the back side of the carpet. Sewn with matching thread into a channel in the pile, the stitches will be hidden by the pile. As an alternative, you can simply glue the binding to the carpet on the back side.

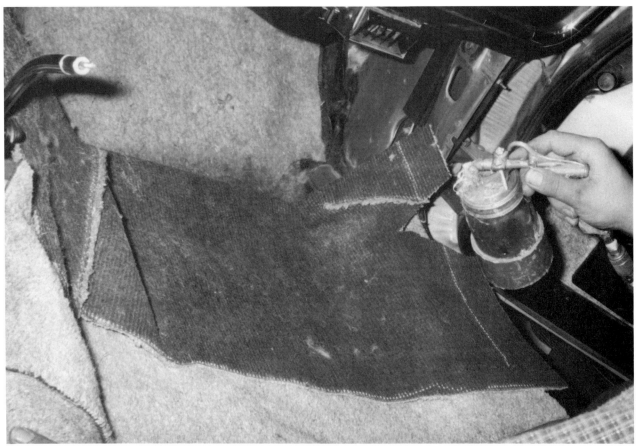

Bind any exposed carpet edges. Put the carpet in place and check the fit once more. Then fold back the front half and coat the back side and the floor or padding with adhesive.

Installation

Cementing the padding to the floor, then cementing the carpet to the padding makes the neatest installation. If either is left loose, it will move around and soon look like a wrinkled towel. Molded and ready-made carpet comes with jute padding attached, making installation a one-step operation. You'll find it easier to install the padding first. Then lay the carpet into position on top of it to make a final check for fit.

Following the same procedure as with the padding, fold back half of the carpet, apply cement to both surfaces and smooth the carpet into place. Repeat the procedure with the other half. The cement will remain tacky for some time in case you need to pull it up and refit. Cement heel pads or any other inserts into place if that hasn't been done already. Tuck the edges underneath trim panels where necessary, and reinstall the door sill plates, pedals, and other hardware.

Finish up by vacuuming the carpet and spraying on a protectant to help keep it clean.

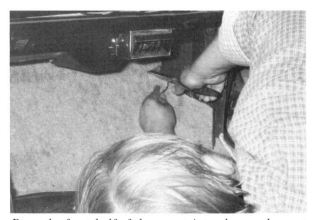

Press the front half of the carpet into place and repeat the process to cement the other half. Tuck carpet neatly into corners and edges. Trim as necessary to make the carpet lie down neatly. Replace the kick panels and door sill plates to hide the edge of the carpet. Use an awl to locate screw holes.

Of course, Fords in 1951 didn't have a neat trunk compartment like this, but if you aren't worried about strict authenticity, a spare tire cover and carpeting on the floor and sides make it much nicer for luggage and picnic supplies.

Chapter Eleven

Other Components

The interior is full of smaller parts, some painted, some plated and others upholstered. We'll try to cover—in the verbal sense—the latter in this chapter.

Kick Panels

These panels under the dashboard forward of the doors often go unnoticed—unless they're really shabby! Besides finishing off that area, they hide wiring and insulation and in some instances contain fresh air vents or storage pockets. Many original kick panels were not upholstered, only painted to match the interior color scheme. On older models they were made of fiberboard, but on later cars are usually molded plastic.

Backyard customizers and, lately, manufacturers have found the kick panels a good place to install stereo speakers. If you are updating the sound system in your car or truck, you may want to do likewise. Such non-original additions can be hidden behind woven cloth upholstery and the

These kick panels with original style pockets are part of LeBaron Bonney's Model A upholstery kits.

If there's no original panel to serve as a pattern, make one of the area to be covered out of heavy paper and transfer it to panel board. Cover and finish the panel as you would a door or quarter panel.

Most package shelves were upholstered with plain cloth or vinyl or not at all. A rolled-and-pleated cover like this one was popular in the sixties and wouldn't be out of place on a fifties or sixties car.

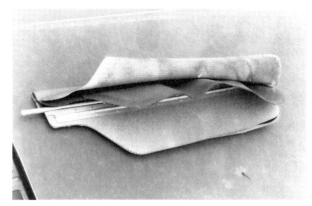

The edge binding has let go on this sun visor, and the cardboard lining is warped, but the Masonite board is still good. You can nearly duplicate the factory construction with cardboard and a new vinyl cover cut, fitted and glued over the base board.

A better solution is new sun visors if they're available for your model. These 1951 Ford Victoria visors are from LeBaron Bonney.

sound will still come through. In the case of vinyl, trace the outline of the speaker onto it, then work out a neat geometric design and punch small holes with a leather punch so the sound can come through. The holes will be barely visible on dark material. Of course, if original appearance is not important, go ahead and install the speaker grilles or even fancy radio grilles from a junkyard relic.

Kick Panel Construction

Remove the original panels and check their condition. Unless they're rotted or warped from moisture, you can probably reuse them. Panels that are broken, cracked, or butchered can be repaired by gluing a piece of panel board onto the back, or fitting it into a hole with a piece behind to hold it in place. Applying a light layer of padding under the fabric covering will hide the repair work.

If new panels are required, trace around the old ones onto a fresh piece of panel board, or make a pattern out of heavy paper or light cardboard. Cut out the panel and trial-fit it in place. Punch or drill any holes required for attachment screws or clips. Any cutouts that are necessary can be made with a utility knife or saber saw.

Upholstering

Installing upholstery on kick panels is similar to that of other essentially flat sidewall panels. You can upholster panels that were not finished that way originally. Use cover material to match the other sidewall upholstery. Padding will lend a fuller appearance, but it's optional.

Lay the panel on a sheet of foam, trace the outline, and cut out the foam. Position it on the panel and hold half in place while folding back the other half. Apply adhesive to the panel and foam and smooth the foam into place. Repeat with the other half. As an alternative, you can apply cement to the panel and the sheet of foam, lay the panel on the foam, then cut around it, leaving just enough foam to roll over the panel edge.

Lay out the cover material face down and trace around the panel board with at least an inch to spare on all sides. Glue the fabric on as you did the padding. Check to see that it's straight and even. Then with the panel face down, stretch the fabric over the edges and glue it on the back. Work from the center of each side out to the corners, checking often to see that it's smooth and neat. Fold the material or cut wedges if necessary to make it lie smooth on the corners. Follow with staples around the edge as insurance against the cement losing its grip.

Mark and cut out any holes for accessories and hardware, folding the edges in and gluing them on the back. Attach accessories and hardware, and install the panels in the original manner.

Remove the old covering and padding, and sand the area to be covered to remove any remaining glue and foam. Photo courtesy of Special Interest Autos Magazine

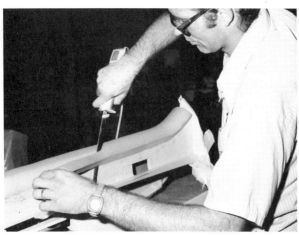

Trim and shape foam to the contours of the dash. One-inch foam was used on heavily padded protruding edge of this Chrysler dash. To finish the foam, trim sharp edges to achieve smooth, rounded contours and sand the foam smooth with 40-grit sandpaper. Photo courtesy of Special Interest Autos Magazine

Package Shelf

Package trays, as well as kick panels and many other miscellaneous interior components, are reproduced for many popular models. If they were upholstered originally, the reproductions are upholstered with a choice of original fabrics or vinyls and ready to install. Unupholstered panels come die-cut to fit as the originals. Check with the suppliers listed in the Appendix.

Chances are the package shelf behind the rear seat wasn't upholstered to begin with. They were often left as painted fiberboard. But covering one isn't hard to do, and it will give the interior a more finished look, if you don't mind departing from the original. With a present-day miracle material like Velcro, it's possible to equip your car with a remov-

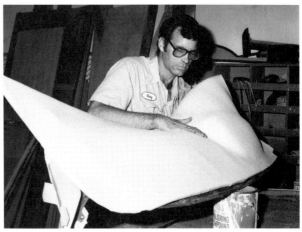

Glue 1/2in foam to the rest of the dash that wasn't covered initially. Work the foam carefully around curves and indentations, and trim all the edges back to leave at least 1/2in for the vinyl to adhere to. Taper the edges with a razor blade, and cut out any holes for radio speaker, defroster, or air conditioner outlets. Photo courtesy of Special Interest Autos Magazine

Here's the dash with foam padding in place. Photo courtesy of Special Interest Autos Magazine

able package shelf cover, to be taken out when the car is being judged for authenticity.

Rolled and pleated Naugahyde package tray covers, especially in candy stripes, were a fad of the fifties and sixties. Such a treatment would be in keeping with that era, and people's choice judges will love it! Colorful rolls and pleats really stand out under the greenhouse-like rear windows of those days.

Almost any cover material can be used to coordinate with the other upholstery. Late-model cars have a carpet-like material. If you install stereo speakers below the package shelf, headliner fabric or any woven fabric will hide them without impeding the sound. Plain vinyl looks good and is easy to install. Refer to the discussion of kick panels earlier in this chapter for how to punch speaker holes in vinyl.

Heat and moisture condensation have often rendered the composition board package shelf wrinkled and rotten, so you may need to make a new

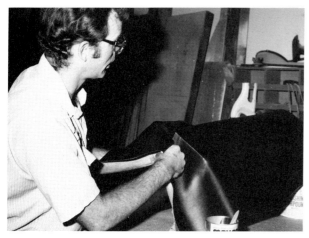

Cut a piece of vinyl large enough to cover the dash with several inches to spare. Glue one end to the dashboard metal, then pull it tightly and glue the opposite end. Check tautness by stretching it front to back at the lowest point. If it is slack or wrinkles appear near the center of the low spot, the vinyl isn't tight enough from end to end. Photo courtesy of Special Interest Autos Magazine

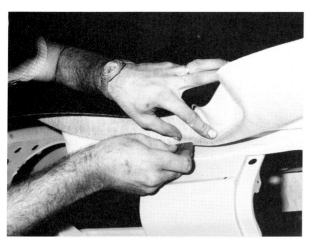

Stretch the vinyl over the front of the dash and mark the area that contacts the dash. Apply contact cement to the marked strip of vinyl and to the corresponding area on the dash. Allow it to set up until tacky. Photo courtesy of Special Interest Autos Magazine

one. Removing the rear seat back should reveal how to get the old shelf out. Trace around it onto a new piece of panel board and cut it out with a saber saw.

A light padding of foam is optional. Cut your cover material an inch or two larger than the board, glue it on the front, then pull the edges around and glue them on the back side. If the tray is concave, as many are, be sure to get a good bond on the top side. If you go for a roll-and-pleat or button tufted cover, make it up following the techniques covered in Chapter Six. Refer back to the earlier discussion of kick panel upholstery for more detail on installing the cover.

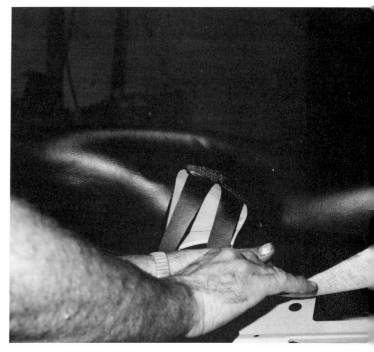

Stretch the vinyl tightly over the dash and glue it down. The cuts shown relieve stress as vinyl is fitted around tight curves. Photo courtesy of Special Interest Autos Magazine

Note how the shelf is installed as you take it out. On some installations the front edge of the cover material is left loose, then glued to the steel shelf platform after reinstalling the shelf. That helps hold the shelf tight and rattle free.

Sun Visors

Because the upholstery has to be installed over a rigid base and finished on both sides, recovering sun visors will try anyone's patience. I'd recommend taking them to a professional trimmer, except that they hate to do them, too! Your ragged visors might still be sitting on his back shelf six months later. One trimmer suggested, "Cover the front, staple it on the back, then install them so tight no one can pull them down!"

Fortunately, visors are among items reproduced for many cars, so you can make an end run around this problem. You may be able to clean the original visors and restitch, if necessary, through the original holes.

If new upholstery is called for, duplicating the original technique exactly may be impossible in a home shop, but here's a method trimmer Norm Kyhn recommends. At the core of the sun visor is a Masonite board, which is stiffer and stronger than upholstery panel board. It is usually stapled to a tube which swivels on the shaft that attaches the visor to the roof. If the Masonite is damaged or broken, cut a new piece to the cor-

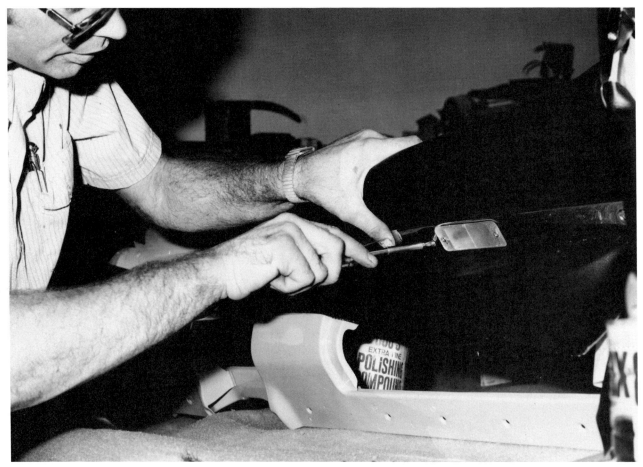

Install the trim along the glued edge to hold the cover while the glue sets up. Photo courtesy of Special Interest Autos Magazine

rect shape and attach the necessary hardware.

Cut one piece of chipboard (lightweight cardboard, like cereal boxes are made of) to cover both sides of the Masonite plus a little to spare. Score and fold it around the Masonite like an envelope, and trim the three open edges even with each other 1/2 to 3/4in outside the edge of the board. Cut the cover material (usually the same vinyl or cloth as the headliner) to cover the cardboard plus an inch to fold and glue over each edge. If the original visors were padded, glue a layer of foam over the cardboard first, or use foam-backed material.

Fold the upholstered cardboard over the Masonite and glue the edges together. If necessary, trim the cardboard where the shaft goes through and tuck and glue the ends of the cover in neatly.

The edge can be left as is, glued together, or finished off with a binding strip, as many originals were. Sewing on binding so it looks neat on both sides is tricky, so take your time. An alternative, although not original, is to install a U-shaped plastic binding trade-named Trimlox. A pinch-type, snap-on windlace originally used on foreign and

sports cars and a few American models, it is available in eight colors to add a neat, finished edge to your recovered sun visors.

Dashboard Recovery

When recovering the dashboard, it's almost mandatory that it be removed for adequate access. If the windshield is being replaced, work on the dash may be possible while it's out. Photograph or make notes of where everything goes.

It's doubtful the dash cover can be kept intact to use as a pattern, but salvage a piece from a protected spot to match the color and grain of the new material.

Remove all the old covering and padding; scraping, sandpaper, solvents, and/or a wire brush may be handy to clean the surface. If you go to bare metal, refinish it with primer or paint.

Cut, fit, and glue on foam padding to duplicate the original form. The leading edge probably had a double thickness, so put that on first and shape it with an electric carving knife or coarse sandpaper. Glue a layer of foam over the entire panel. If you

138

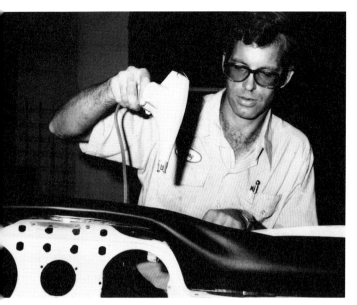

Heat the vinyl carefully with a heat gun or hair dryer to soften it. Photo courtesy of Special Interest Autos Magazine

Starting at the lowest point, stretch the vinyl over the forward edge. Take your time (this step could take an hour). About one hundred pounds of pull are required. If possible, have a helper apply heat to the vinyl while you pull. Photo courtesy of Special Interest Autos Magazine

have to piece the foam, put duct tape over the seams so they won't show through. One dashboard restoration specialist uses half-inch closed-cell landau top padding for the final layer, hand sanding it to shape with forty grit paper, then on down to 180 grit to form a perfectly smooth surface. Taper the edges, and leave at least a half inch of metal for the vinyl to adhere to. Cut out holes for speakers, defroster ducts or other attachments. If any holes necessary in the cover might be hard to locate, insert a small washer in the padding so a magnet can locate the spot later.

Make a pattern from remnants of the old cover, if possible, or with heavy paper or scrap fabric. Allow plenty of extra on all sides when cutting the new material; on this job you need enough to get a good grip to stretch it over the panel. Trial-fit the cover to the dash and mark the center or other reference points. Set the material in the sun (assuming vinyl) to make it more pliable. With contact cement, glue one end to the dash, stretch it tightly to the other end, check the alignment and glue the other end. Hold the back (windshield) edge of the cover while stretching the front edge and mark the strip where glue is to be applied. (Do not glue the cover to the foam.) Apply contact cement to the marked strip on the cover and the dash surface, and when it's tacky, stretch the vinyl tightly and glue it down. To work the vinyl around tight curves, make vertical cuts to relieve stress. Immediately install trim to hold the glued edge in place, even if you have to take it off again later.

Pull the cover to the back edge and mark it for gluing; you should be able to glue the cover over the edge for additional strength. Apply cement and

stretch the cover into place, working on the more contoured areas first. A heat gun or hair dryer will help keep vinyl soft and pliable. An extra pair of hands will be useful to get a good, strong pull on the cover as you glue it over the back edge. Take your time to get it straight, tight and smooth. You don't want wrinkles to appear as it relaxes with time.

Allow the glue to set up well, then trim the edges. If an edge is covered with a trim strip, trim the vinyl to the center of the attachment holes. Cut out holes for speakers, etc. Make a series of cuts around the perimeter, and fold and glue them underneath so the cover won't pull loose. Replace the hardware and reinstall the dash in the car.

Door and Side Armrests

Up through the mid-fifties, armrests were a separate piece attached to the door, usually with a couple screws. As interiors became more stylized, the armrests were integrated into the door panel, but often the armrest base can be removed separately after the door trim panel or covering is removed. Armrests at either end of the rear seat may be formed wood or metal, padded and upholstered. The rear seat backrest will likely have to come out for access to the attachment points.

Remove the old cover and use it as a pattern to cut new cover material for a door-mounted armrest. Renewing the padding may involve gluing on a layer of 1/4 or 1/2in foam to form a smooth surface; cutting out damaged sections of padding and gluing in new foam; or removing the old foam and

139

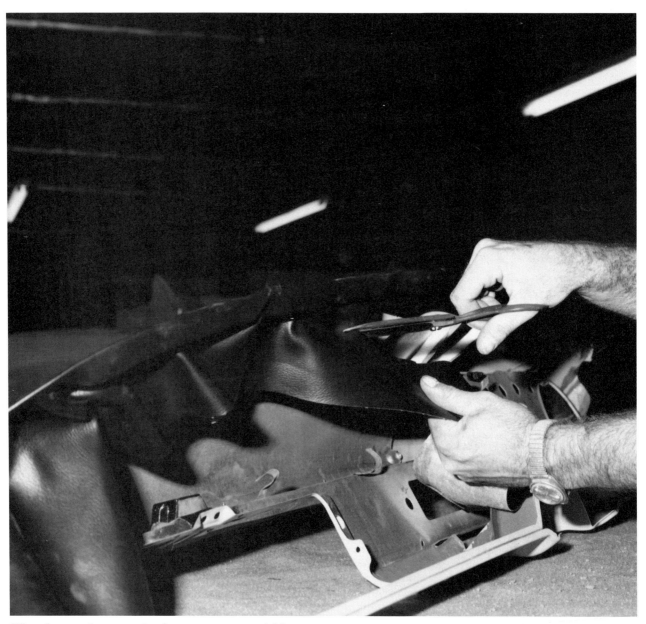

When the cover is secure, trim the excess cover material from all edges. Photo courtesy of Special Interest Autos Magazine

replacing it with new. A medium- or high-density foam was often used to pad armrests, which can be shaped, if necessary, with coarse grit sandpaper.

If the bottom of the armrest is out of sight for example, a fabric-covered pad attached to a base you can glue the cover fabric on. Make *V* cuts as necessary to fit it tightly around the curves and to avoid bunching on the bottom. Heat vinyl carefully with a hair dryer to help stretch it around the armrest. U-shaped armrests found on cars up through the mid-fifties may require painstakingly hand-stitching the cover onto the armrest for a neat, smooth finish. Notice how it was constructed originally as you remove it; it

may be one piece of material or two sewn together. Carpet binding makes a good reinforcing strip to give strength to the seam. Try clamping the piece in a vise between two boards to compress it while stitching so the cover will be smooth and tight when released.

Padded armrests at either end of the rear seat in models from the thirties to the fifties were often constructed like seat cushions with layers of cotton padding and a pleated or tufted cover. Others were merely covered with upholstery material to match the seats or side walls.

With the back seat and upper rear quarter panels out of the car, you can determine how the

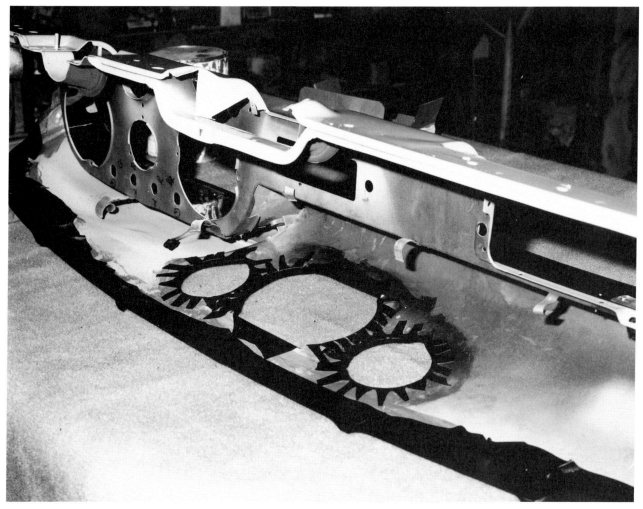

Cut out the vinyl in the center of the speaker and defroster holes, then slit the edges of the openings. Fold these edges in and glue to the inside of the dash. Photo courtesy of Special Interest Autos Magazine

armrest panel comes out. Remove it and take the upholstery off. Replace or renew the padding if necessary. Make up new covering, using the old for patterns. This is a case where the armrests on opposite sides are probably mirror images, so leave one intact as a model while you work on the other.

Seat Armrests

The armrest integrated into the front or rear seat should be treated as a separate unit. While disassembling the seat, remove the armrest; the rear seat backrest may need to come out for access to that one. Remove the covering, noting how it is constructed and attached. It will probably be similar to the seat on a smaller scale: a cover made up of two or more pieces, maybe different fabrics, sewn together with welting in the seams for strength. Inside there may be a spring structure supporting layers of binding and padding, or, on a less elderly vehicle, a molded foam insert.

As with other parts, cut the cover apart and use the pieces to cut new material to shape and size. Renew the inner padding. Then as you assemble the new cover, check it often for fit. When installing the cover, turn it inside out, put a thin sheet of plastic over the foam padding so it will slip on easily, then gradually roll the cover down over the padding. A smooth dowel rod can help in adjusting the cover, and steam, either applied to the outside or by a wand inserted under the cover, will help remove wrinkles and shrink the cover into a snug fit.

Storage Pockets

Auto designers have occasionally provided storage pockets in various places—door panels, kick panels, or in the back of front seats. We covered the procedure for making pockets in Chapter Seven, where they were installed in the seat backs of a 1949 Hudson convertible. If you have storage pockets to do, refer back to that section.

With instruments, wiring and trim reinstalled, the dash is ready to go back into the car. Photo courtesy of Special Interest Autos Magazine

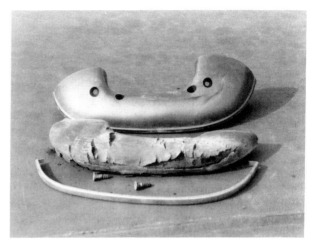

A typical armrest in the fifties was a molded foam top with a fabric or vinyl cover attached to a plastic base. To recreate it, cut a piece of Masonite to shape, glue on foam and trim and sand it to shape. Make a cover of the correct material, put it on tightly and glue or staple it to the board.

 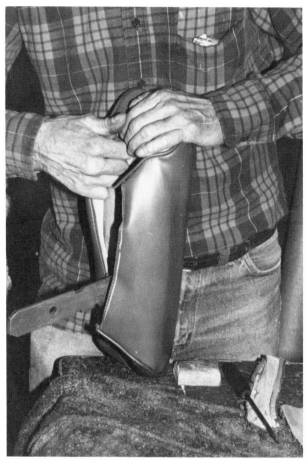

The center armrest cover is integral with the seat cover in this Cadillac. Redoing one like this requires taking the cover apart at the seams and using the old pieces as patterns for cutting, fitting and assembling a cover of new material.

Moe Wilson used the old center armrest as a pattern for making this new headrest cover.

Chapter Twelve

Convertible Top

With his Model T and subsequent Model A, Henry Ford put a new car within reach of the common man. One or two generations later those two long-running series put a restored antique within reach of the common man.

The enthusiasts of the fifties and sixties were often those who had grown up driving and working on Model T and A Fords and now wanted one again to recapture their youth. And the most desired body style was the roadster. Its jaunty looks and freedom of open air driving made the roadster the restorer's preferred model. Subsequently, the cabriolet or convertible became and has continued to be the sought-after model of later generations.

The popularity of the T and A models also started the reproduction parts business. Thanks to

LeBaron Bonney makes roadster and convertible tops for Fords and Mercurys from Model As through the early fifties.

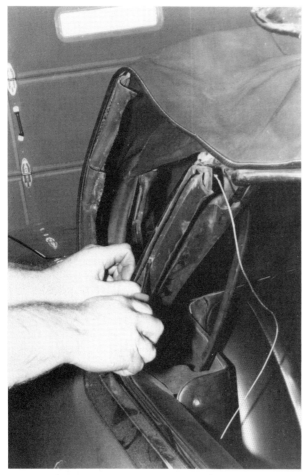

Randy Vajgrt of McVicker's Auto Upholstery and Tops demonstrates the installation of a replacement convertible top on a 1966 Cadillac. His first step is to loosen the top at the windshield and remove the weather strips that are screwed onto the window channel.

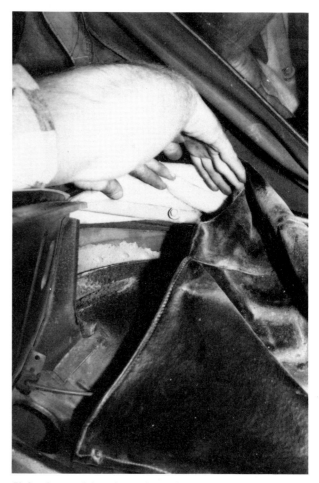

Take the top fabric loose from the header. On this Cadillac it pulls over the header and staples on the under side. At the back, the top, window curtain and vinyl well liner all attach to a tack strip that bolts into the body. For access to the bolts holding the tack strip, take the well liner loose from the rear seat back. One of the tack strip bolts is visible here. Next, pull the corners of the top loose from the tack strip.

that, there's now an industry providing a multitude of components to make restoring all kinds of cars easier, including convertible tops.

Made-to-fit tops are available for most cars, which places the job of top replacement within reach of the home hobbyist. Few would attempt it if they had to make up the top covering themselves, but we'll include the basic instructions in this chapter, along with steps for repairing and replacing the convertible top.

Top Repairs

Before diving into installing a new top, take stock of the one on the car now. Can it be repaired satisfactorily to provide a few more years of service? Sometimes seams let go when the thread wears out and only need to be sewn together again. Minor rips or tears can sometimes be repaired by gluing a patch of the same material on the inside. Sewing will make the repair stronger, but would have to be done by hand unless you remove the top. Repairs will be more successful on tears running lengthwise of the top, but it's difficult to make repairs to tears running across the top hold because of the tension when the top is up.

The rear window and surrounding curtain can be replaced separately, saving a lot of work if the rest of the top is good. The main covering is usually made in three sections, so it can be taken apart and a new section sewn in, but the savings in time and money would not be great.

Choosing a Replacement Top

Ready-to-install tops are available in a variety of materials to duplicate and, in most cases, improve upon the original while retaining the authentic look. Convertible tops need replacement every few years, so don't assume the one that's on your car is original. If in doubt, research the correct material before starting.

Haartz cloth, a cotton canvas material made by Haartz Manufacturing, is made to original specifications and is said to be the most original material for pre-1955 convertibles. Outer and inner layers of water repellent cotton are bonded with a layer of rubber between. Other trademarked materials duplicate the original feel and texture of the original cotton canvas but contain synthetic materials that are more resistant to fading, staining, shrinking, and sagging. Tops for later models are also offered in original equipment-grade vinyl or heavier, more durable material that looks the same.

Check the top framework carefully and try to determine the cause of any tears or worn spots. There may be tacks, staples or bolts protruding. Sometimes the side rails get out of alignment and can pinch the cover when the top is raised or lowered. The pads that protect the canvas cover from direct contact with the framework and give the top a smooth look may be worn out. You'll probably want to replace them along with the top.

On early cars the top covering was tacked to wooden bows attached to the steel folding framework. Replacement bows, if needed, are available from antique suppliers for popular makes, but may have to be custom built for rare models. Save whatever remains for patterns.

Repair and refinish the top framework and power lift mechanisms, and make sure everything works smoothly before beginning installation of the new top.

Bow pads are usually included when you order a new top. If not, they can be made of material to match the inside of the top, folded double or triple with a layer of foam or other padding sewn inside. There's usually an indentation in the bows that the pads fit into to give you the width. They tack or staple to the header and, on some cars, to the rear bow, on others to the rear tacking strip.

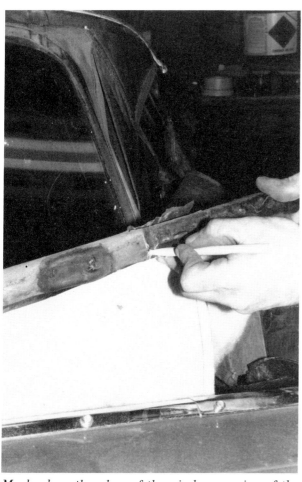

Mark where the edges of the window opening of the main top panel and of the window panel contact the tack strip so you can line up the new top in the same position.

Removing the top cover exposes the staples holding the back window panel to the rear bow. Remove them and take out the tack strip with the window panel and well liner attached.

Separate the window panel and the vinyl well cover from the tack strip. In this case the well cover will be

reused, so Randy scrubbed it thoroughly with vinyl cleaner and reattached it to the tack strip.

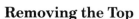

Align the new window panel with the tack strip. Use the center point and the marks you made on the tack strip. Trim away the vinyl material around the holes for the bolts that hold the tack strip to the body.

Measure the distance from the rear bow to the middle of the rear body opening. This measurement (usually furnished with the replacement top) is critical for everything else to fit correctly.

Removing the Top

Methods of attaching the top to the body in the back and the header in front vary from make to make and year to year, so take careful note of how yours was installed. On Model A Fords and other early cars the top is tacked to wooden top bows and tack strips around the edge of the passenger compartment. Top bows on later cars are steel, and the canvas or vinyl cover attaches to composition tack strips only in the front bow, or header, and around the rear of the body opening.

While Randy pulls the window panel as tight as possible, Matt staples it to the rear bow. This method is necessary to avoid any slack in the panel.

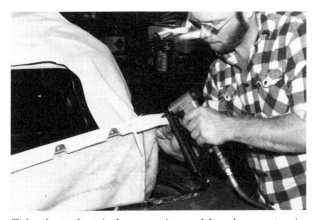

Take the tack strip loose again, and lay the new top in position. The rear corners should have holes corresponding with the tack strip bolt holes. Line them up and check the alignment of the window opening with the marks you made on the tack strip. Staple the corners of the top to the tack strip, then bolt the tack strip back into the body.

Randy temporarily glues the front of the top cover to the header with the top partially open, then closes the top and fastens the header at the windshield. This holds the top taut while the cover is fastened to the rear bow. Drive a few staples to hold the top cover to the rear bow and create a straight line across the top. Next, staple wire-on welting to the rear bow. Trim, fold over, tap it smooth with a body hammer, and screw on the metal tips.

149

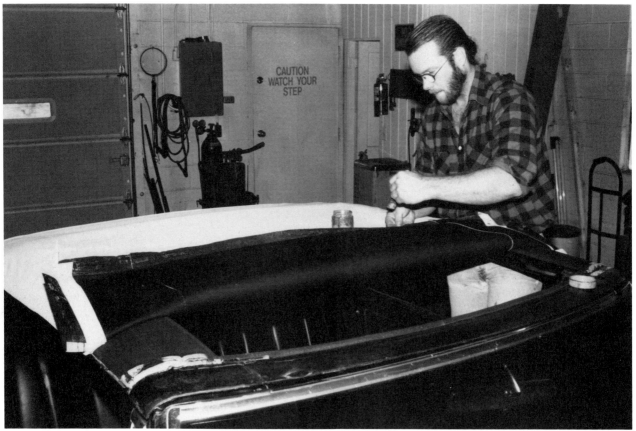

With the top still in the "up" position and latched at the windshield, mark a line where the top cover pulls over the edge of the header. Unlatch the header from the wind- shield and take the top cover loose from the header. While the cover is loose, feed the cables that hold the top down on the sides through the listing strips sewn into the top.

Apply cement to the front edge of the top cover and to the header. Use the reference line you made previously to adjust the tension of the cover as you glue it to the header. If it was taut and smooth before, pull it about a half inch further over the header. The vinyl will stretch over time, so get it as taut as possible now.

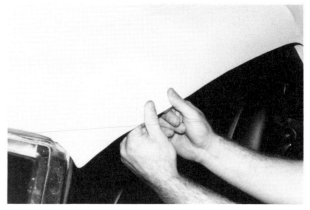

Latch the top in the "up" position and pull down on the sides to remove any wrinkles. If it should be too loose, go back and reglue the header to add more tension. Pull the back corners tight and glue the flaps to the top frame behind the quarter windows. Fold the top down and trim the excess material.

Cut a length of rubber windlace core to stretch across the header, and fold it into a strip of vinyl. Sew the core into the vinyl strip leaving one side of the flap wider than the other (this should be provided with the replacement top).

Open the flap and staple the narrower side to the inside edge of the header. Pull it smooth as you staple across. As with welding, tack it first with a few staples, then go back and staple at 1/2in intervals. Fold the corners back neatly and secure them with staples. Finally, glue down the top portion of the weather seal flap.

Raise the top from the windshield and remove the weather-strip from inside the header bow. Some are screwed on, others are glued and must be pried loose. This weather-strip isn't provided with a replacement top kit, so save the old one to put on or buy a new one. Remove the weather-stripping around the quarter windows—it holds the top cover to that portion of the frame—and any other fasteners along the edges. Put fasteners and hardware where you can find them easily. Remove the metal tips on the wire-on welting over the rear top bow and then the welting itself. It should be tacked or stapled to a tack strip in the bow. With the wire-on removed, the tacks or staples holding the top and rear curtain to the rear bow will be exposed and can be removed.

Take the top canvas loose at the front by removing the staples attaching it to the header bow. At the back most tops are stapled to a tack strip which, in turn, bolts into the body. On older models the tack strip may be outside the body and the edge covered with welting or a molding. Sometimes the top well liner must be removed to provide access to the tack strip, sometimes the liner also attaches to the tack strip. Remove the tack strip from the body and mark reference points on it where the rear window curtain and the corners of the top attach to help position the new pieces properly. Remove the rear window curtain. It is a separate piece that attaches to the rear bow at the top and the tack strip on the bottom, or it may be a curtain or plastic window that zips directly to the top. The new window and panel come as a unit ready to install.

The top cover may be attached to the second bow to keep it from ballooning at speed. If so, either a piece inserted into the bow must be detached by removing screws and the insert piece removed from a listing strip attached to the top, or the entire bow is taken loose and slid free from the listing strip.

Preparing the Framework

The rear top bow must be in the correct position for everything to fit right, so measure from the back of the body opening to the middle of the rear bow before removing the pads. Suppliers often provide this measurement with the replacement top. Many tops also have webbing strips, which hold the bows in position relative to each other and provide a foundation for the pads and covering. Repair or replace both webbing and pads as necessary, stapling them to the header and bows or rear tack strip as on the original installation.

When all the pieces that attach to them have been taken loose, check the condition of the rear tack rail and tack strips on the header and rear bow. If yours are still serviceable, be sure all old tacks and staples are removed. If they are breaking up to the point that they won't hold staples well, replace them. New tack strip material sold by various suppliers is better than the original material, or you can make your own. Cut strips of composition board the correct width, glue them together to create the correct thickness, and attach them with pop rivets. Old fan belts can also serve as a tack strip.

Making a New Top

The main top covering is usually made up of three separate pieces. The center panel extends from the header bow to just behind the rear bow, overlapping the rear window curtain, or in some cases all the way to the rear body edge with the window curtain cut out of it. The side panels run from the header to the rear corners of the body opening and from the center panel out to the window line. These sections are joined with heat-bonded seams on later tops, but since that requires special equipment, they can be sewn, as on earlier convertibles.

Split apart the pieces of the old top and use them as a pattern for the new one. If it has stretched or shrunk noticeably, take that into account. If there is no top fabric at all, take careful measurements from the top framework and mark them on the new top material. As they say, "Measure twice and cut once"—and allow plenty of extra material around the edges. It can be trimmed later.

The distance from the header to three or four inches past the rear bow will be the length of the center panel. The outer panels run from the header to the rear tack strip and flare out to the corners around the rear quarter windows. Allow at least four inches of width for seams, six to eight inches of length for tacking.

Draw the center line on the material before cutting out the center panel. Cut out the side panels and lay all three sections in place for a rough trial-fit before continuing.

The edges of these panels will be doubled over and joined together with a triple sewn seam 1/2–1in wide to provide strength and a smooth, weather-tight seal. Lay the center panel and one side panel face to face, the edge of the center panel an inch inside the edge of the side panel, and sew a seam 1/2in inside the edge of the center panel. Fold the edge of the side panel back on itself, lining up the fold with the edge of the center panel, and turn the center panel face up, making a fold an inch wide. Sew through all four layers 1/4in inside each fold. Repeat the procedure to sew the other side panel to the center panel. Lay the covering over the top bows to check the fit and mark the side edges for finishing.

The sides of the top are usually reinforced and finished with a binding. Cut pieces of top material 1 to 1-1/2in wide to follow the window line. Sew them inside the edges of the top with the seam about an inch in from the edge. Then sew on a matching binding to cover the edge where the two pieces come together.

Add any other attachments that were on the original top, such as listing strips to hold the top down to the second bow, sleeves along the edges for cables or snaps to hold down the sides of the top. After checking the top for fit, double over and sew the edges that will attach to the tack strip. The double thickness will give the tacks or staples a better grip.

Making the Rear Window Curtain

Manufacturers first used small glass back windows in convertibles, then went to larger, clear plastic windows in the fifties. Later, some returned to glass. The small glass windows were usually contained in a two-piece metal frame. A plastic window may be sewn directly to a zipper that allows it to be opened before the top is folded down, or sewn into a canvas panel that zips to the top. On some later convertibles the glass or plastic window may be bonded into the rear curtain. You'll have to determine the method used on your car and proceed accordingly. It may be that you'll need to remove the window, zipper, or both and use them in a new panel.

The easiest window replacement is a plastic window sewn into a canvas curtain. Half of the zipper is sewn to the edge of the curtain and the other half to the top. If only the window needs replacement, you can leave the top in place. Using the old curtain as a pattern, cut the new curtain out of matching top covering material, and cut out the window opening. Cut out another strip 1-1/2in wide in the shape of the window opening, and cut the window plastic to size. Sandwich the plastic between the main curtain and the reinforcing strip when sewing it in, and finish the edge with binding as was done on the sides.

Reinstall the weather-strip moldings on the sides of the top.

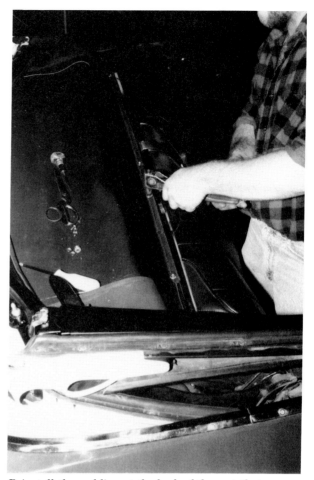

Reinstall the molding at the back of the seat that secures the front of the well cover. Some moldings have the male half of snaps to attach the boot cover, some have an awning rail the boot cover slides into and still others use Velcro.

Line up the center of the zipper with the center of the curtain. Starting at that point, sew around in one direction, then return and sew in the other direction.

For a plastic window without a curtain, the plastic is cut to shape and the zipper sewn directly to the edge of the window in the same manner. Heavy-duty clear plastic material can be obtained from auto trim suppliers. To avoid scratching it while working, tape heavy paper or cloth over it.

Installing the Top

Steps in installing the new top should be the reverse of how it was removed. You'll be able to tell in what sequence the individual pieces were installed. Generally, those on which the rear window or window curtain zips to the rest of the top, the main top goes on first. Then the window is zipped into place and the bottom strip attached to the rear tack rail. If the rear window curtain contains both halves of the zipper, the curtain will probably go in first and attach to the rear bow underneath the main canvas. That type of installation is illustrated.

Use the center point and the reference marks you made on the tack strip to line up the new rear window panel, and staple it to the strip. If necessary, trim material away from the tack strip attachment holes. Reinstall the tack strip with the window panel attached into the body.

Another set of hands will come in handy to pull the window panel taut as you staple the top of the panel to the rear bow. Staple the middle first, followed by the outer corners, then go back and staple solidly across. Don't be afraid to take staples out and redo them if the panel is wrinkled or too loose. Now is the time to get it right; it's tough to correct later.

Remove the tack rail from the body again and lay out the main top covering. If it's designed for a specific model, it should come with holes for the tack rail screws, which help line it up on the tack rail. If not, position the top cover by your reference marks, staple it to the tack rail and punch the holes. Reinstall the tack rail in the body.

Pull the front of the top over the header bow, glue it temporarily and latch the header. That will put some tension on it while you staple the covering to the rear bow. Wire-on is the fabric-covered trim strip that covers the row of staples on the rear bow. Measure where the ends were on the old top, a few inches outside the top seams, and trim it to length. After you staple the wire-on into place, it folds over itself to hide the staples. Tap it down smooth with a body hammer. Pierce the fabric with an awl and screw the metal trim tips over the ends of the wire-on.

If the top is now taut and wrinkle free, mark where it folds over the header bow in front, then unlatch the header and put the top halfway down. Loosen the front. There may be side cables that hold the sides of the top down tight. Insert them through the listing strips provided inside the edges of the top. There may also be a listing strip that glues to the inside of the top and attaches to the front bow to prevent the top from ballooning. Install it now, too.

Apply cement to the rear quarter window area of the side beams and the rear corner flaps of the top. Pull the flaps tight as you glue them to the side beams.

Take the top loose from the header again and apply a new coat of adhesive to both header and top fabric. It was probably not as tight as it could be when it was glued temporarily, so pull it a little tighter now, pulling the reference marks you made an additional half inch or so over the header. Then put the top all the way up and latch it at the windshield. It should be uniformly tight with no wrinkles. Remember the top will stretch with use, so get it tight now. Reinstall the rear quarter window weather-strip moldings, which also hold the rear corners of the top securely.

Fold the top down all the way, putting the header in the top well where it's easier to work on. Finish off the front corners smoothly by folding it and stapling the material, and trim the excess material inside the header. Along with the rubber weather-strip that attaches to the inside of the header, there is a water seal finished to match the top, which may not be provided with the top. To make it up, cut a strip of rubber windlace core and sew it into a strip of the top material. Open up and staple the inside flap to the inside front of the header. Fold the corners back and staple them down smoothly. Glue down the top portion of this flap.

Reinstall the molding on the back of the rear seat that holds the front of the top well cover. Some have snaps to hold the boot cover, others have an awning rail the boot cover slides into, and still others have Velcro for attachment. Apply steam to remove any remaining wrinkles in the top. It will tighten as it cools.

The Top Well Liner

Often the top well liner is simply a piece of vinyl attached to the back of the seat and to the rear tack rail. If it needs replacement, use the old one as a pattern to cut and sew a new one. Some convertibles have removable, upholstered panels. In this case, proceed as you would for side panels, cutting new boards as necessary and covering them with the appropriate material. As in other areas, the key is noting how these parts were assembled and installed originally, then duplicating those processes as closely as possible.

Quarter trim panels, surrounding the top mechanism at either side of the back seat, may be constructed and upholstered in a variety of ways. Some are sheet metal and must be finished in the car. The most common covering will be vinyl, which is cut to fit and glued on with a light layer of 1/2in scrim for padding.

Other convertibles may have composition board panels in this area, which can be removed and reupholstered out of the car. Later models have molded plastic panels which may or may not have an upholstery covering. Reproductions of these are available for popular models.

The Boot Cover

If you were able to buy a ready-made top for your convertible, the same supplier probably also makes a reproduction boot cover. Designed to protect the top when it's folded and present a smooth, finished look to the open car, the boot cover was usually made of fabric to match the top on earlier cars. Along with vinyl tops, vinyl boot covers to match the top of the interior upholstery came into use in the mid-fifties.

Early convertible or roadster tops were quite bulky when folded and rested outside the car body. Boot covers for these are more like an envelope or sack completely enclosing the folded top. Later convertible bodies incorporate a well for the top to fold into, with the boot attaching to the rim of the body and the back of the seat.

The front edge of the boot cover may have a welt that slides into an awning rail attached to the seat, or it may attach with snaps. Some later models also use Velcro fasteners. The cover usually snaps around the sides and back to a stainless steel trim strip. In the sixties some manufacturers began using nylon tabs that slip under the molding.

If you need or want to make your own boot cover, use your convertible's old one as a pattern. It will likely be made up of one large piece with separate smaller pieces sewn to it to cover the side rails. Make note of how the seams are finished, then separate the pieces. Trace around each piece onto new material, allowing extra for seams and to fold in to make a strong, double thickness edge.

Apply steam to remove any wrinkles. Steam heats the vinyl, which will tighten as it cools.

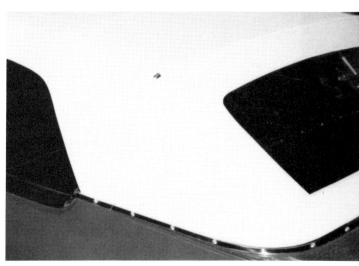

With the new top completed, Dan Buckner's Cadillac convertible is ready for many more years of enjoyment.

In the event the boot cover is missing, make patterns out of heavy paper or cloth. It would probably be worth your time to make up a complete cover out of a material such as muslin and check it for fit before duplicating it in vinyl or top fabric.

Sew the individual pieces together following techniques outlined previously. In many cases a welt is sewn into the seams for strength. If in doubt, include it. Welt cord may need to be sewn into the leading edge to fit into the awning rail.

Fold the edges back and sew a seam one to one-and-a-half inches in, then sew a binding to finish off the folded edge.

Fit the boot cover to the body and, pulling it taut, mark the locations of the snaps on the trim strip. Install the female part of the snaps to the cover, centering them in the doubled edge.

If you have some material left over, you may want to sew up a pouch to store the boot cover in when not in use.

Appendix

Upholstery and Supply Sources

General upholstery fabric, material, and supply firms are found generally in larger cities. Most of them are wholesalers who deal only with established trim shops. It may be helpful to develop a relationship with a local trimmer, who can help you obtain materials that aren't available from other sources.

Auto restoration has become such a popular hobby that it now supports many businesses which supply all kinds of mechanical, body, and interior parts. Many of these companies provide everything for a few makes and models, while others specialize in interior products for a wide number of vehicles.

Exact reproduction fabric, panels, and even complete reupholstery kits are offered for popular models such as Mustangs, Model As, and 1955–57 Chevys, while for an uncommon model you may have to settle for something reasonably close to original.

Following is a list of some firms that handle upholstery and interior supplies. I have listed, in general, the products they offer. Remember that they are continuously adding new products to keep up with changing demands in the restoration market, so if you don't see the specific item or car model you're interested in, contact those that handle something along the same line; they may have added what you need. Bear in mind that companies dealing in NOS fabric have such a turnover in stocks, depending upon demand for certain materials and their ability to uncover new stocks, that even they may not know from day to day what ones they can supply.

Parts Suppliers

Acme Auto Headlining Company
P.O. Box 847
Long Beach, CA 90813
Phone 1-800-288-6078
   Replacement and custom headliners and headliner installation kits, windlace, side panel fabric, carpet, vinyl, and convertible tops, well liners, and boot covers

American Supplies
13444 Belle River
Riley, MI 48041
Phone 313-395-7312
   Upholstery materials for sixties Ford, Mercury, Comet, Mustang, Thunderbird, Falcon, and Fairlane; carpet, convertible tops

AMX Connection
19641 Victory Blvd.
Reseda, CA 91335-6621
Phone 818-344-4639
   Carpet kits for 1968–70 AMX

Auto Custom Carpets, Inc.
P.O. Box 1167
Anniston, AL 36202
Phone 1-800-633-2358
   Original-style carpet, floor, and trunk mats

Auto-Mat Co., Inc.
225A Park Ave.
Hicksville, NY 11801
Phone 1-800-645-7258 (orders) 516-938-7373 (information and in NY)
   Upholstery kits and materials for U.S. and foreign cars and trucks; carpet, seat covers, side panels, dash pads, headliners, convertible tops

B-D Company
1361 S. Broadway
Denver, CO 80210
Phone 303-744-1405
   Carpet, vinyl, and convertible tops, dyes and vinyl repair kits, tools, and supplies

C.A.R.S., Inc.
1964 W. 11 Mile Road
Berkley, MI 48072
and
904 Rancheros
San Marcus, CA 92069
Phone 1-800-521-2194 (orders) 313-398-7100 (information)
   Upholstery kits for Chevrolet, Camaro, Chevelle, Monte Carlo, Nova, and Chevy pickups; original or custom seat covers, headliners, door and side panels, armrests, sun visors, carpet, convertible tops and boots, trunk mats, dash pads, and supplies

Chevyland Parts & Accessories
3667 Recycle Rd.
Phone 916-638-3906 1-800-624-6490 (outside Calif.)
1-800-624-8756 (in Calif.)
   Upholstery kits and supplies for Camaro, Chevelle, Corvette, Nova, and Chevy pickups; seat covers, headliners, door panels, carpet, dash covers, sun visors, trunk mats

Ciadella Enterprises, Inc.
3757 E. Broadway, Suite 4
Phoenix, AZ 85040
   Original and custom upholstery kits for 1951–83 Chevrolet, early Corvette, and Chevrolet pickups; seat covers, door and quarter panels, headliners, carpet, convertible tops and boot covers, sun visors, trunk mats, and other supplies

Color-Plus
P.O. Box 404
Kearny, NJ 07032
Phone 201-659-4708
   Leather and vinyl reconditioning and recoloring products

Hampton Coach
P.O. Box 665
Hampton, NH 03842
Phone 603-926-6341
   Complete upholstery kits and individual seat, headliner and panel kits and convertible tops for most 1916–54 Chevy and 1931–53 Buick models and some Plymouth, Pontiac, Cadillac, and Oldsmobile models

ICP Crown, Inc.
624 Valley St.
Lewistown, PA 17044
Phone 1-800-288-6874 or 717-242-2730
Interior products for Camaro, Chevelle, Nova, Cutlass, Firebird, GTO/LeMans, Fairlane, Mustang, and Thunderbird models; seat covers, door and quarter panels, carpet, headliners, convertible tops, and other supplies

Juliano's Interior Products
321 Talcottville Rd.
Vernon, CT 06066
Phone 203-872-1932
Original and custom upholstery kits, fabric, leather, carpet, headliners, seat covers, padding, and insulating material, supplies

Kanter Auto Products
76 Monroe St.
Boonton, NJ 07005
Phone 1-800-526-1096 (orders) 201-334-9575 (information)
Upholstery kits and components for U.S. cars 1928–80; seat cover kits, headliners, windlace, carpet, fabric and leather, convertible tops, supplies

LeBaron-Bonney Co.
P.O. Box 6
Amesbury, MA 01913-0006
Phone 508-388-3811
Interior kits for Ford and Mercury, 1928–54; seats and covers, side panels, headliners, soft top kits, convertible and roadster tops, side curtains, fabric and leather, carpet, upholstery tools, and supplies

Legendary Auto Interiors, Ltd.
121 West Shore Blvd.
Newark, NY 14513
Phone 315-331-4444
Upholstery kits and supplies for Chrysler Corp. products, 1963–76; seat cover kits, door and side panels, headliners, carpet, sun visors, convertible tops, supplies

Motor City Originals
16094 Common Rd.
Roseville, MI 48066
Phone 313-774-4949
Upholstery kits for Dodge Coronet, Challenger, Charger, Dart and Plymouth Belvedere, GTX, Road Runner, Satellite, Barracuda and Duster; seat covers, headliners, carpet, door panels, sun visors, dash pads, convertible tops, and other supplies

Mustangs Unlimited
185 Adams St.
Manchester, CT 06040
Phone 1-800-243-7278
Upholstery restoration components for 1965–73 Mustangs, some Cougars; headliners, carpet, door and side panels, seat covers, sun visors, dash pads, trunk mats, installation hardware, carpet for 1974–93 Mustang

National Fabric Co., Inc.
Phone 1-800-821-7542
Full line of upholstery fabric, supplies and tools; wholesale only—call for referral to the nearest retail outlet

National Parts Depot
3101 SW 40th Blvd.
Gainesville, FL 32608
Phone 1-800-874-7595 or 904-378-2473

Upholstery kits and supplies for 1964–72 Chevelle, 1967–81 Camaro, 1955–57 Thunderbird, 1965–73 Mustang; seat covers, door and quarter panels, vinyl and convertible tops, sun visors, carpet, trunk mats

Original Auto Interiors
7869 Trumble Road
Columbus, MI 48063
Phone 313-727-2486
Upholstery fabric and vinyl (NOS yardage for 1950s–1970s models); molded carpet, trunk mats, 1958–66 Thunderbird seat covers, carpet, door panels, headliners, convertible tops, and supplies

Parts Unlimited, Inc.
12101 Westport Road
Louisville, KY 40245-1789
Phone 502-425-3766
Wholesale only; write or call for referral to a nearby dealer; upholstery kits, seat covers, headliners, door and side panels, convertible top pads, wells and boots

Quality Sewing
224 W. Third St.
Grand Island, NE 68801
Phone 308-382-7310
Portable walking foot industrial sewing machines

SMS Auto Fabrics
2325 SE 10th Ave.
Portland, OR 97214
Phone 503-234-1175
Upholstery fabric for American (and some foreign) cars, 1930s–1980s; fabric, vinyl, leather, headliners, carpet, some seat covers and door panels, trunk lining

Steele Rubber Products
1601 Hwy. 150 East
Denver, NC 28037
Phone 1-800-544-8665 or 704-483-6650
Weather-stripping and other reproduction rubber items for car and truck restoration

L. Walston Auto Interiors
37435 Porter
Lucerne Valley, CA 92356
Phone 619-248-7345
Upholstery kits and components for cars 1928–up; seat covers, headliners, windlace, original and reproduction fabric, carpet

J.C. Whitney & Co.
P.O. Box 8410
Chicago, IL 60680
Phone 312-431-6102
Upholstery kits, seat covers, headliners, carpet, convertible tops, tools, and supplies

Year One, Inc.
P.O. Box 129
Tucker, GA 30085
Phone 1-800-950-9503
Interior restoration supplies for muscle car era GM and Chrysler cars; seat covers, door and quarter panels, headliners, carpet, dash pads, trunk mats, sun visors, hardware, and supplies

Clubs and Associations

Owners of particular makes and models band together in clubs for mutual support and enjoyment of their vehicles. Clubs offer a great deal of help to anyone restoring one of the vehicles. Magazines and newsletters carry historic information and photos, as well as want ads to help locate needed materials. National clubs usually have regional affiliate organizations, which can give you contact with owners in your area. Club gatherings are an opportunity to inspect vehicles similar to yours and talk to the owners about correct restoration procedures. Often, a club will sponsor the reproduction of parts, including upholstery materials, most needed by the members.

In the following list, the first five organizations are devoted to vehicles of all makes that meet a certain criteria. The remainder of the clubs listed are for specific makes and models. This list is by no means all-inclusive; it covers the principal clubs for most makes. Contact the ones that apply to your restoration project and see what help they can provide.

Antique Automobile Club of America
P.O. Box 417
Hershey, PA 17033
    50,000 members; library and research center

Classic Car Club of America
2300 E. Devon Ave. Ste. 126
Des Plaines, IL 60018
    Certain 1925–48 luxury and specialty models; 5,000 members

Contemporary Historical Vehicle Assn.
314 Alyssum Circle
Nipomo, CA 93444-9208
    Vehicles 25 years old back to 1928

Horseless Carriage Club of America
128 S. Cypress St.
Orange, CA 92666-1314

Milestone Car Society
P.O. Box 24612
Speedway, IN 46224
    American and foreign cars 1945–72

American Motors Owners Association
6756 Cornell St.
Portage, MI 49002

BowTie Chevy Association
P.O. Box 608108
Orlando, FL 32860
    1955–57 Chevy cars and trucks

Buick Club of America
P.O. Box 401927
Hesperia, CA 92340-1927
    Buicks from 1903 to 12 years old

Cadillac-LaSalle Club, Inc.
3083 Howard Rd.
Petoskey, MI 49770

Chevrolet Nomad Association
8653 W. Hwy. 2
Cairo, NE 68824
    Chevrolet Nomad station wagons 1955–57

Classic Chevy International
P.O. Box 17188
Orlando, FL 32860
    Chevrolet cars and trucks 1955–57

Early Ford V-8 Club of America
P.O. Box 2122
San Leandro, CA 94577
    Ford Motor Company vehicles 1932–53

Hudson-Essex-Terraplane Club, Inc.
P.O. Box 215
Milford, IN 46542

Kaiser-Frazer Owners Club, Inc.
P.O. Box 1251
Wellsville, NY 14895
    All Kaiser, Frazer, Henry J. Kaiser Darrin, Willys, and Graham vehicles

Late Great Chevys
P.O. Box 607824
Orlando, FL 32860
    Chevrolets 1958–64

Lincoln & Continental Owners Club
P.O. Box 68308
Portland, OR 97268
    All Lincoln and Continental cars

Model A Ford Club of America
250 S. Cypress
LaHabra, CA 90631

Mustang Club of America
P.O. Box 447
Lithonia, GA 30058

National Antique Oldsmobile Club
P.O. Box 915
Fremont, OH 43420-0915
    Oldsmobiles through 1964

National Corvette Owners Association
900 S. Washington St.
Falls Church, VA 22046
    All Corvettes

National Corvette Restorers Society
6291 Day Road
Cincinnati, OH 45252-1334
    Corvettes 1953–77

Oldsmobile Club of America
P.O. Box 16216
Lansing, MI 48901

The Packard Club
P.O. Box 2808
Oakland, CA 94618

Packards International Motor Car Club
302 French St.
Santa Ana, CA 92701

Plymouth Owners Club
P.O. Box 416
Cavalier, ND 58220

Pontiac-Oakland Club International, Inc.
286 Ahmu Terrace
Vista, CA 92084

Studebaker Drivers Club
P.O. Box 28788
Dallas, TX 75228-0788

United States Camaro Club
P.O. Box 608167
Orlando, FL 32860

Vintage Chevrolet Club of America
P.O. Box 5387
Orange, CA 92613-5387

Vintage Thunderbird Club International
P.O. Box 2250
Dearborn, MI 48123-2250
    Thunderbird cars 1958–66

WPC Club, Inc. (Chrysler Products)
P.O. Box 3504
Kalamazoo, MI 49003-3504
    Chrysler, Imperial, DeSoto, Dodge, Plymouth, and Maxwell

Glossary

Acrylic: a synthetic fiber with good wear characteristics found in upholstery fabrics, especially as the surface fiber in a pile weave.

Batting: matted cotton used for padding and filling upholstered pieces.

Backrest: the back or upright portion of a seat.

Bench seat: a seat with a cushion extending the full width of the passenger compartment. A split bench is two individually adjustable sections without space between.

Blind stitch: a hand sewing technique started on the underside of the cover fabric; sewing thread is not visible on the finish side.

Broadcloth: a strong, flat fabric made of cotton, rayon, or wool once widely used for auto upholstery.

Burlap: coarse jute cloth used to cover springs and support the padding.

Bucket seat: a seat designed and (usually) contoured for one person.

Button tufting: a finish style with covered buttons inserted through the cover and drawn down into the back to create raised areas called tufts.

Channel, channeling: see Tuck-and-roll.

Coil spring: a wire seat spring formed into a spiral.

Cotton: a fiber made from the cotton plant, woven into fabric. Also cotton batting, a mat for padding and filling upholstered pieces.

Cover: the outside or surface material on an upholstered piece.

Cushion: the horizontal, sitting surface of a seat.

Dacron: trade name for DuPont's polyester fiber used for a variety of fabrics; also applied in mat form as padding or filler.

Density: the measure of the stiffness or compressibility of foam.

Embossed: a fabric design raised from the surrounding surface.

Fabric: a cloth made by weaving, knitting, or felting fibers.

Fiber: a fine, threadlike filament or matter composed of filaments.

Finish: the quality and appearance of the outer surface of an upholstery material.

Foam: a spongy, cellular, urethane-based material for shaping and padding upholstered pieces; short for foam rubber.

Headliner: the inside roof covering of a vehicle.

Hidem: a finishing strip stapled over a seam with two thin welts which close to hide the staples.

Hog ring: a C-shaped steel wire fastener with sharp ends used to attach material to a seat frame or wire.

Hog ring pliers: a tool with jaws designed to hold a hog ring and crimp it around a seat frame or wire.

Indentation load deflection (ILD): a measure of the hardness of foam expressed in pounds.

Kick panel: the panel ahead of the front doors below the dashboard.

Listing strip: a fabric sheath attached to a cover through which a wire passes to hold the cover.

Masonite: a pressed wood fiber sheet, one of several types of material used as panel board.

Mohair: fabric made from Angora goat hair, characterized by a thick, medium length nap. Once a popular upholstery fabric, it has generally been replaced by synthetic materials with a similar finish which are sometimes referred to as mohair.

Nap: the short, fuzzy ends of fibers on the surface of cloth.

Nylon: a synthetic material capable of assuming a variety of forms including cloth thread and fibers, known for its toughness, strength, and elasticity.

Padding: the resilient material—usually foam, cotton, or Dacron—which provides fullness and softness to an upholstered piece.

Panel: any of the several pieces making up the auto interior, most of which are upholstered, or a component of a cover.

Panel board: composition board providing a form for upholstering.

Pile: the upright looped or cut fibers on the surface of a fabric; applied especially to carpet, but also referring to cover fabrics.

Pleat: a fold of even width, usually sewn or stapled with a hidden seam.

Quarter panel: usually the interior panel behind the doors, or the rear quarter section of the vehicle.

Roll-and-pleat: see Tuck-and-roll.

Scrim: muslin-backed foam used as a backing for constructing seat and panel covers.

Side panel, side wall: panel or panels covering a side portion of the interior. A side panel usually refers to any such panel except a door, while side wall refers to the side panels collectively.

Sinuous spring: seat spring made of heavy-gauge steel wire with zigzag bends, also called zigzag, NoSag, and sagless.

Stay tack: attaching material temporarily with widely spaced tacks or staples for fitting or alignment. Tacks are not driven all the way in.

Tack stitch: a temporary stitch to hold materials together for fitting or alignment.

Topstitch: sewing from the top side of the cover material through the padding, resulting in a visible seam.

Tuck-and-roll: a finish design in which the cover is padded and shaped into a series of rounded, tubular sections (rolls) with tucks (pleats or channels) between; also called "roll-and-pleat" or "channeled."

Tuft: the puffy, raised section created by drawing down depressions in the surface of an upholstered piece; the process of making tufts.

Tweed: a coarse cloth in a variety of weaves and colors.

Velour: a fabric with a thick, soft nap or pile; the French term for velvet.

Velvet: a fabric with a thick, soft pile or nap.

Vinyl: in upholstery, a fabric made of a coating of plastic (vinyl) over a knit or woven cloth backing.

Wadding: matted cotton or other material used as padding or filler.

Warp: yarns running lengthwise in a woven fabric.

Welt: a cord of fabric used for decoration and to add strength to a seam.

Windlace: a fabric-covered roll forming a seal around door openings.

Wire-on: a finishing strip stapled over a seam which folds over itself to hide the staples.

Woof, weft: filling yarns running across a woven fabric, interlacing the warp yarns.

Index